# The Fox and the Dark Apple of the Dancing Herd

**Poetry by Bruce Owens**

Published by Imagination Earth LLC

**Imagination Earth LLC**
**455 Market St Ste 1940**
**PMB 319628**
**San Francisco, California 94105**

*The Fox and the Dark Apple of the Dancing Herd*

This edition was first published by Imagination Earth LLC in 2025.

Cover Design by Devin Masterson
Editing and Formatting by Devin Masterson

The Fox and the Dark Apple of the Dancing Herd

ISBN: 979-8-218-62590-0

*Imagine, Design, Create!*

*"I took the colors of silence and painted a moon on a moving curtain."*

- Bruce Owens

Select poems in this collection have appeared in previous works by Bruce Owens.

*Quiet Places*

*A Passage Through Stone*

*Mend The Broken Branch*

*Eddies in the Rush*

*Across the Light*

# Acknowledgements

I want to thank those who have helped me throughout the years to bring this collection of poems together. Thank you to Janine Pickett and Andrew Sivak who provided the endorsements for this book. Special thanks to my friend Devin who worked with me to complete this project.

# CONTENTS

# Foreword

By: Devin Masterson

Bruce Owens is a rare and shining example of what it means to live a beautiful life – spreading joy through his words and embodying a heartfelt grace. His life's work has been foremost within his own heart, and the love he cultivates overflows into the world through his poetry. As a devoted writer and seeker of truth for over 50 years, Bruce is one of America's great wisdom keepers, and it is my honor to provide the foreword to his latest collection of original poems.

One winter evening, Bruce and I met serendipitously just as the Roaring Camp Christmas Train was passing by the Neary Lagoon at twilight. The train full of revelers had slowed, and Bruce, with his white beard and blue eyes, turned his electric wheelchair to wave a jolly "Ho, Ho, Ho, Merry Christmas!" My girlfriend and I adored his Santa Claus charade, and the train full of passengers celebrated with glee. It was quite a magical first impression by this community elder. We stayed to hear his stories of life in the 1960's – like when Jerry Garcia stopped Bruce in Berkely on Telegraph Avenue to invite him to a rooftop show with the

Grateful Dead. We were intrigued by the lore of long ago and when Bruce asked if he could recite his poem "Wife", we happily obliged, now curious about this charming old fellow who had a playful wonder about him. Bruce then enchanted us with the mystery and poetic romance that only a master could deliver. He invited us to stay in touch as we said our farewells and we walked home arm in arm with our hearts aglow.

Several months later, by chance – or perhaps via divine grace – Bruce and I found each other again. I stopped my bike to see Bruce on his loyal electric steed sporting blue iridescent sunglasses, a tan, and white bandages on his legs. I asked him how he was doing, to which he replied that he was happy to see me again, but was in pain from a lingering wound and could use some help at home. I visited him that night to help around his apartment and read poetry. We just clicked as they say. This was the beginning of a spiritual friendship and mentorship that has carried us both through my coming of age and his navigation of aging. I later learned that Bruce was a fixture of the Santa Cruz community, known for reciting his poetry from memory to folks from all walks of life and stopping to pray for those down on their luck.

Bruce was hospitalized that year and had to bear the healthcare system, while I would visit to sneak in his favorite snacks and wildflowers. We would meditate and read poetry together as Bruce sought to transmute his suffering into humor, poetic wisdom, and spiritual growth. At the hospital, Bruce had me bring him a book written by his teacher he simply referred to as "the Monk". We began to read the

Western Monk's writings on Buddhism and Christianity before meditating, then discussing our experience and insights on the teachings, and finally praying together for Bruce's healing. Thankfully, Bruce made his way home and slowly recovered to continue his studies, prayer, and of course capturing poetic insights. I began to understand Bruce's mystical embodiment of Christ's teachings and his study of Buddhism as an almost Blakean gnosis. His poem "Chocolate Pudding" on page 44 was written from his hospital bed and captures the glimpse of a joyous and nostalgic revelation amidst a painful time.

Bruce told the story of how he met the Monk walking in robes down The Strand in Manhattan Beach, CA. He shared that the Monk taught him how to meditate and enjoyed his poetry, even providing critiques. The Monk was an Oxford-trained linguist who studied seven languages in his education and was said to have spoken up to seventeen different languages when he passed. He worked as a film translator in Hollywood before renouncing the Western world, traveling to India, and devoting himself to spiritual practice. Bruce was quick to admit that he admired the Monk's wisdom and was most grateful for the time they shared. The Monk spoke to Bruce about faith and scripture, carefully respecting Bruce's beliefs while saying that he would only discuss Buddhism if he asked.

The Monk's no-nonsense attitude to life and his expertise in language helped Bruce to develop spiritually and hone his chosen profession of writing. Mr. Owens recalled a story of reciting a poem to the Monk to which he replied: "Well, that was a nice lightshow. Now let's hear a poem!" Bruce said that his teachers didn't have mercy on him, challenging him to keep writing, but to do so powerfully without fluff. This relationship and the Monk's teachings can be found in the reverence of Bruce's mystical poetry, where he balances transcendence with concise language and a love for the mystery of creation.

As Bruce and I grew closer, he began to share stories of his influential relationships with William Everson, Thomas Pynchon, and the Polish Nobel laureate Czesław Miłosz. Bruce once met Miłosz, who was recognized as a humanitarian and one of the greatest poets of the 20th century, at a poetry reading in San Francisco. Bruce later sent a handwritten letter to Miłosz and was delighted to receive a reply, beginning their short correspondence over poetry. The writings of Miłosz opened Bruce's mind to the greater world of poetry and awakened him to the human struggle for freedom.

William Everson was a disciple of Robinson Jeffers, literature professor, and world-renowned hand press printer, who became a teacher and friend to young Mr. Owens. Bill was the beloved poet-in-residence at U.C. Santa Cruz and taught a course aptly named *The Birth of a Poet*. His original hand press printings are now featured in the Huntington Museum in San Marino, CA. Bruce recalled organizing a field trip for students in the Y.E.S. Program to visit William Everson's home and learn about writing. Bruce's passion for the craft made him a torch bearer that carefully passed the light of writing to the next generation. Owens admits that he was intimidated when he first visited the famed Everson's home by pointing to an aged photograph of Bill's

Kingfisher's Flat studio along Big Creek in Santa Cruz. The same humble demeanor with twinkling eyes that led Bruce to these friendships can be felt within the intricacies of his poetry.

Mr. Owens also developed a friendship with the mid-century novelist Thomas Pynchon, known for *Gravity's Rainbow* and *The Crying of Lot 49*. Bruce told me a story of visiting Pynchon to receive feedback on his short stories and poetry. Pynchon didn't pull any punches; he said no one in America knows how to use a semi-colon and then critiqued Bruce's historical fiction storyline. However, he noticed that Owens had accurately employed Italian geography and culture, then asked how he did it. Bruce replied that he had found an old Italian travel book and studied it to build the scenes, to which Pynchon admitted that he secretly used the same trick. Bruce thanks these teachers for their wisdom and encouragement to "keep writing" as he sought to hone his craft, just as a stream polishes a stone.

Lastly, I must mention that Bruce has spent time teaching young adults healing from addiction and abusive homes how to rediscover themselves and their inner peace through the art of poetry. He has also guest lectured on the power of creative writing at colleges throughout California including Cabrillo, and spent a year teaching in Oklahoma, paying forward the gift of poetry that has given him so much. May this collection of treasured poems provide you with the same touch of grace that Bruce has so lovingly bestowed upon the world.

-*DM*

*"I want to awaken the word in awaken."*

- Bruce Owens

# A Kind of Tango

Her skin glows under the light of fireflies.

Her voice is a wounded bouquet thrown on the sea,

and her eyes,

those eyes are like a voyage that never ends,

an exploration of light,

where a whole continent rises

from the water of the orchid.

The earth is on fire with an invisible music

that is gathering flowers from the eyes of children,

and the earth, our dear earth, is balancing

on the edge of a word,

and soon will spill into eternity,

but her laughter out here

on the porch, in the evening, glows

with the hues of a moth,

mingles with the cicada,

and is blue like the song

of a nightbird.

Her face, that lovely face is wet with the moon,

but so much solitude in her face,

and in that face, everything shines.

Even the blemishes of her face are like a rare flower.

Her lips are both tragic and faithful,

and when they fall on my body,

her lips talk to me of far-off islands,

an oasis trapped in a bottle

like a diamond,

and finally, her lips tell me about the bee's sting

in the storm along the coast.

In the latitudes of fire,

tropical fish are the lanterns in her dreaming hands,

and her touch to my lips

is a silence that shapes a dream.

She rests in my shadow as I rest in her shadow

on these cool summer sheets

that are like trickling ferns

in the dark by the open window

framed by the oceanic pulse of waves.

It is all like a Tango that kills as it gives life,

this dance between us, this bliss that covers us

like a soft rain that soon departs

like the seasons of this Earth.

# After Reading a Poem
# by Our National Bard


I want to yank his low-lit cranium
glowing from within as if it were a lamp
on a desk in his study,
"where his cat is slumbering on the sofa"
and walk him politely through a village in Cambodia
or take him into a war-torn town in Bosnia
and have him seated at the table
as dinner is being served up politely
as the depth of winter outside
closes in on this small family
that offers our "versifier"
the last of their wine and bread
as they eat their neighbor's dog.

Our versifier, no doubt, would remark
on the distinction of the wine
as he engaged these dislodged creatures
in conversation
from the armchair
of his dense lifestyle insulating him

in a sort of Boschian bubble
as in "The Strawberry Painting."

I'm certain they would be impressed and intrigued
as he sampled their wine and engaged their minds
with his story telling
and "perceptions about California lowlife"
and the particulars of a jazz junky's life
in the late 50's.
There is no "salmon-colored poodle named Banjo"
and if the animal had existed
in this landscape without heat
it would have added flavor to the hot soup.
But yet,
the jazz junky sold his poodle for a quick fix.
Everyone at the wooden table nodded
not out of understanding,
but from an inbred politeness.
There was no electricity
and one of the oil lamps flickered from a draft.

Our versifier seemed to wrestle with inquisitive bees
and "a rendezvous with a vile ant"
in a California climate where blue sky
lapped at the lawn

and he anticipated the martini
at "the cocktail hour with the soft blaze
of an alto sax as background music."

I would that the ancient lettering of ogham
with notches for vowels should cut
deep into the placid landscape
of our "national versifier"
and that the clever lines of our friend
would fathom the deep wells of the fili
and he would stretch out
in a clearing on the forest floor,
hands tucked under his head
and watch the hawk hovering overhead
as a swarm of wild bees covered his naked body,
nuzzling his skin as if it were a white flower.

We are waiting for those new poems,
poems that will stretch out over us
like an Irish landscape rolling to the edge
of a sheer crag and drop us down
into the foam of a wild ocean
that even the moonlight cannot tame,
nor the clever lines of academia.

# Almost

You can almost
touch the breathing of your lover,
hear the ocean stirring in there,
where her life is drawn in
and breathed out.
You can almost
hear the surf lapping
on the shore of her dreams
while her heart drums softly.

Her nerves are threads of clear silk
embroidered into a cloud
that drifts above her skin.
You can almost see
the shadow of the cloud
as it sails into the harbor.

It is summer in her body.

The gold ring on her finger
glows like a sunset.
You can almost wear it,

but the splendor of love
slips below the horizon
and the day leaves us
to memory that almost
allows us to catch what is lost.

# Angels

Angels peer into my dream,

breathless,

blue shadows in clear slips;

a face turns, and smiles.

# Appearing

The shells on the window sill
glow with the morning.
It is late morning. She is asleep.
She is breathing softly.
A hummingbird at the window stares into my life,
then disappears.
There is all this disappearing
and reappearing in life.

I wonder if the hummingbird at the window
was trying to recognize me by my eyes
or simply looking for red hues in flowers
and seeking the nectar buried
at the heart of the Fuchsia.

She is awake and yawns.
The morning has disappeared
into a cloud outside the window.
I smile at her as she sits up in bed.
Her eyes seem to recognize me
and then that look of love appears,
a small wonderful glow appears.

# __Apple__

A bite into an apple
takes me
into
October
where the days have shortened into
something sweet,
and as the orchard enters me;
I become
golden,
and delicious
in the translation of the seasons.


I touch the apple skin, and it sings my skin.
The apple is a map
that guides me
to a place
I have never been.
There is
a distance
inside the apple
I have never crossed.

Perhaps, someday,
I will make that journey, and find
the village lights
of the firefly.

# A Snowflake

Asleep in a flake of winter rain,
that has frozen into something intricate
but not so mysterious nor intricate
as the eyes of the woman, asleep
next to me, on a soft bed, the color of snow
that sifts along under a cold moon.
We have lived in the big city for over a year.
It has been snowing all night.
The power is out.
There is no electricity.
The entire city is quiet.
I light one small candle.
The flame is quiet.
I only hear her breathing lifting up,
ever so lightly, then falling
like a flake of snow,
falling slowly now, quietly, we are sleeping
as the snow falls outside the window,
dusting the city with white pollen.

# Aster

Most
people live on a flat earth.

They see cruise ships, tankers spilling off
the edge of the ocean
in the currents of a huge waterfall.
Those
that live in high-rises
have but a contained vision.
Only
the astronauts experience
the true beauty as they peer down
on the small blue marble, streaked with white.

I walk in the woods alongside a stream
and listen into the murmur of divinity.
I carry within me the eyes of the astronomer
and see the woods punctuated with aster
and other wild flowers.

# A stone is

a pregnant wind,

and the wobble of water lives within.

Outside is

a ring of granite the mountain wears.

The wild is adrift with leaves.

Westerly winds turn the current

and trees bend with the fury

that has come in from off the Pacific.

Clouds shadow the hills

as they sweep along the coast in passing.

Winter sleeps in the bottom of a well,

sleeps in the still cold water.

But a fire is burning down in the deep

and begins to awaken all that sleeps,

and begins to awaken all that sleeps.

# A Woman's Hope

No moon.

The wind sleeps

on the water.

Inland lake sea birds chatter in the dark.

Night is on the lake.   It is late.   No sky.

Just the stars dreaming on the currents.

The lake is wide and long and has no mouth

to speak its weight of water.

October.

Cold.

Black oaks drop acorns,

a resonance
in
the hollow
slips
to the floor of the woods,
looking to sprout in a new season
like a middle-aged woman,
divorced, hoping in the night
with her head on the pillow,
that Spring will fulfill her longing
for touch and a new relationship of warmth.

# Astounded

I was astounded...stunned into clarity that reached
past my own face and kneeling

into my own shadow I saw my shadow fall though
the images of my life

and in the light of the keyhole I peered

into your eyes and her eyes and the sweet rain

falling on all of our faces

in the low place

in the high place

valley to mountain

blue to gold

I was astonished

No words found my mouth

No light found my eyes

I have become all light and all sound

and nothing at all

and yet

everything at once

just before sleep

and the last foot fall across the leaves

in the woods asleep

# **Awaken**

It was late.
I could not find my bones.
They had become like blades of grass
lost in the drift of night
or like leaves that had fallen
quietly as a shift in season.
The marrow of my bones was a frozen stream
slipping thru the woods;
a dark signature of my life that for many years slept
in the meandering light of autumn
turned to a winter blaze of ice.
I did not comprehend the thaw of Spring
and that a deeper current always was
the truth of my life.
Fear was my tormentor etched into a clear mirror
and I burned in that cold blaze
and I had memorized that fire of ice.
But the thaw has unleashed a joy
and the signature has awakened to light.
The flesh never could truly tarnish the spirit I am
because Spirit had given birth to spirit
and that life lives eternally within the deeper flow
of who I am.

# Baggage

I walked with her
to the grave of her dead husband;
this ritual of placing flowers
at the foot of a cold erect stone.
I was more interested in the stark trees
that lined the cemetery road.
It was quiet that day.
She knelt over her memories,
And placed fresh cut colors, still in their prime,
on the place
of her mourning.
The earth over his grave
had no concern and paid no attention.
The setting sun had no compassion for her,
and light on the branches
held no memory of the scene.
I felt it odd
that she would not take my hand,
as we walked slowly back to the parked car.

That night as I sipped at her wet body
and lapped into her like a small wave of fire,
she called out his name.
This set a strange boundary between us,
and this was the beginning of our divorce.

# Barbarossa Directive of December 18

Autumn came early to Leningrad.
There was no heat anywhere. Just cold.
No one touched the living bark
of a tree with an ax for warmth.
They would rather freeze than destroy
the loveliness of a beloved place.
On the other hand, one man's half-naked body
was covered with bites. No dogs did this.
The dogs disappeared quickly, even the family pets.

Hollow tanks just twenty miles
from the center of the city:
iced steel stymied on the spot
with no will to retreat or advance.

Nine-hundred days slipping over sabers
like daylight,
and night pressing like barbwire
against the throat of a wolf,
and the child was found
playing with a headless doll.

There was no medication, no light, no water,
no transportation in the winter of 1941,
when the Nazis slit open the belly
of horses and climbed inside for warmth,
waiting out the siege of the city
as the sun climbed over the white glare of ice.
One decimal descent up from this
is the slums of Chicago, New York, Philadelphia,
Cairo Illinois
where the slow barges of the Mississippi slip pass
pockets of poverty, whole towns slump down
on one knee rotting like the stump
of an old tree, and in villages pluvial
enslaved by merchants of the wind
as the Ganges receives
the burning flesh on funeral pyres,
and off in the distance the din of the crowd.
Then there is the poverty that dwells within.

But these Soviets linked their minds to freedom,
and across the frozen Lake Ladoga, the ant line
carried in the supplies.

There are wounds on the heart that remain alive
into the Twenty-first Century
forming a kind of genetic heritage,

a land of its own.
Despite the best efforts of the mind and body,
there is no consolation for these places
in the minds that grow dense
like a black hole in space
or the scar under the scarf near the jugular.
And scars like lichen on the north side of trees,
always there if we should ever get lost in the woods.

If we listen to scars
they tell us of brutal men and women,
and scars act like the needle on a compass
pointing the direction home
even if when we arrive,
we are gathered up in a gunnysack
and tossed into the stars.

All of this gives strength.
The spirit is undaunted, a thing not to be conquered
not even at worlds end nor afterwards
because we will be released
from our scar torn bodies,
snowflakes under the moon,
we will become what we are:
intricate and unique destinies blossoming with light.

There will be huge rents in the gunnysacks
that were lined up
then cramped into boxcars going nowhere.
Everyone will have climbed out from the rent cloth
and have escaped into their own lives,
where tea is served
and the train is a little off schedule,
and bread is served with warm butter,
and the love making goes on
even in the late afternoon.

Then there will be those who
escape of their own bodies,
the freed ones, who will go on living forever
in that place where there is no pain, or sorrow.

# __Beachcomber__

Wind as the indolent scarf. The hum of ocean,
lash wild, and swash of night splayed song;
magnetic male
with majestic might tamed only by her soft
shouldered shores.
The salmon stream cuts up into her soft ferns
as she flows down into him
murmuring in the wound;
the sound in the shallows, the hurt in the hunt,
that slain thing near the edge of memory,
a deer caught in a tangle of brier, and branch,
shot through with an arrow, her soul
stained with pity resting on the evening
like the light before dusk.

The threadbare boulders by the cliffs
are like boned knuckles white with moonlight.
Tussle cry of seabird. Tone tide waves wisp clean
in the hiss along the shore. To walk here
in this slip of water on a mirror of sand.

The clarity catches my mind by surprise
arousing divinity sensed as awe; pure window
on the universe. Out there a buoy.
I shiver against the cold.
Tuck my hands into pockets
woven from the memory of my tribe;
a collective helix,
of digital summation, billions of coda a second
in tenths that spell out sight and sound,
cognition spelled out from childhood in cues
that find rapture in destined arrangements
that fit perfectly in every sector of the brain
sweep of neuronal performance.
It is just the ocean at night with a full moon.
I have lost a name for it.
Call it a vision of this world,
reality at the end of a nerve pulse.
Call it excessive beauty
mixed with the sensation
of time locked into gravity.
It is just one man walking along the shore.
Call it whatever you please, beachcomber.

# Between The Light And The Shadows

And what will I wake with as the moon glides,
unseen in the immense sky folded in on its own day
like a hushed bird turned black by mist?
Will I find my childhood pond,
down the country road,
aglow with the beginnings of a brisk light,
I can never return to,
watch the darkness of the pond water
begin to glow with daylight?
What will I catch
as I awaken on the bed in a room in a body,
some fifty years later.
Even the memory of it
has been shuffled somewhere in time
between shadows and light.
But there still remains a joy in it
as I watch the little boy row out on the water
and cast his line, waiting patiently
to catch the dream that has already passed.

# Black Stone Shining

Walking along Waddell Creek,
a rain starts to sweep in from the ocean.
I spot a small, round black stone.
It glows with its own light.
It has its own music,
there is a magnum opus
about to break out
within the black stone.
To be alone
within this black stone is to touch
the shadow of reality.
Within the stone some stars are beginning to shine
and the cosmos is slowly exploding outward.
I look up and a thin slice of rain
falls on my face.
No one knows the meaning of the black stone
lying alongside the slip of creek
with its winter drive.
The same force that formed the stone
is the same force that drives the creek.
I have been encountered just as I have encountered
I am satisfied to have known the stone,
the moment it held and this time in winter.

# **Buffalo Head**

He wanted to walk off into the frontier,
slip into the sheen of a crow,
and fly, tunnel under the prairie grass,
and disappear into the moist night,
listening under ground
to the stampede of buffalo overhead.
All he wanted was to follow the evening
flow of the Sweetwater, become a shadow
among the stones, count shooting stars forever.

These notions were soon abandoned,
as they built a saloon out in the middle of nowhere.
Then they laid a spur of track out across the dust
so tourists could shoot buffalo
from the windows of the train.
The local Indians posed for photographs
with their newly adopted friends.
The saloon was full of smoke
and smelled of whiskey.
Bowler hats hung on hooks,
and women folk hung onto their bloomers,
and some men folk hung from the gallows
that swayed with heavy shadows.

The Sweetwater mirrored
the arrival of clouds in slow bends
from Devil's Gate
as far as the eye could perceive West.
They would never find the reflection of his face
as he leaned over the water.
No one would photograph
his eyes as they peered down
into the quiet depths of the Sweetwater.
This is all he wanted
when he walked into the frontier;
this was payment enough
to reach down and touch the river running clean.

No buffalo head hanging above
the saloon door to bring him peace.

# **Bullets**

Floating up to us,
flowers

from an undiscovered place

like dreams
in a dressing room, the color of an autumn forest.

But now these flowers are fragrant with gunpowder,
petals of white lead,
and these flowers fly through us
or riddle the stucco of buildings with holes
the size of a child's open mouth.

# **Burnt Toast**

There is some finality to burnt toast.
That clean, soft white bread has lost its vocation
and is burnt black as Johannesburg
is lost to poverty.
We could put burnt toast on a stick
and place it out on a lone stretch of highway
and it would read like a road sign
after a brush fire.

# Can You Hear Them

(for my dear friend Elizabeth Moore)

Should I say something simple like the light
in a bird about to speak?
Can I lift a mountain full of human cries
and toss it into the sea?
I have walked with my solitude
folding my shadow into a leaf...
And this solitude, a scarf wrapped around my words
to keep off the chill of winter, darkening the trees.
I walked the trail one late afternoon,
and talked with a man, who wrote poetry
in his cabin... a dog by his feet.
I told him to read slowly the seasons of his life.
In return, he said, "My road is behind me,
and yet I still stand on it,
and watch the evening turn to dark."

Pull the stars down and watch them swim
in a bowl full of water.
Capture the rose as it turns to dusk
like the lips of that long ago lover.
Place an ear to the stream in the woods
and listen for forever.

This is your time to turn thin as a waiter.

Serve the Master.

He knows

your heart that flowers in a mirror

reflecting a storm that smooths out into a vast quiet.

I hear the children coming through the door,
laughing like water,

and their small faces shine.

Keep this music close to your heart.

Nothing to fear when it all goes dark.

Nothing to fear.

Nothing to fear when it's going towards the light.

Just angels singing.

Can't you hear them...

Singing, that is...

# Canopies

of shifting shade
as I enter the calm hills,
taste the dip of branch
as it touches water.

Each leaf tracing dream
as it falls
with gold
on the skin of a stream.
The oaks are canopies
that cool
the cows with honeyed woe
eyes,
a kindness
in that look
as old as the hills.

I take a cattle trail into the hills
to sit in a dell under the great altar
of an ancient oak.

The whole landscape carries the moon
that spreads light over a still pond.

Crickets fold me into their hum
as I begin to dream the night and the hills.

# Catching Moonlight
# In A Hand-Mirror

I enter the gate of the dictionary
only to discover a cemetery for words.

The headstones are cut with inscriptions
that try to keep something in place
that was lively and hummed in the mouth
like a lump of coal in a furnace of fire.

Some headstones slump over with a cupped ear
listening to the long grass that sleeps at their feet.
Years of rain have eroded the epitaphs
on their small faces and now they stand alone
without meaning, an insignificant memorial
to nothing in particular,

like a pedestrian walking off into the woods
where there is no path.

I close the dictionary gate that clangs shut
like two iron framed windows one can gaze through
onto that world that once was a green park
free of the archaic wolf packs frozen in time.

I live in a world where everything around me
is to be explored
and I am erasing the old entomologies,
listening with excitement as cups and spoons
embark into the mystery where words
are translated into heavenly beings,
alive once more at the tip of our tongue
and I go about the business
of trying to catch moonlight in hand-mirrors.

# Cello

All my life it has been poetry.
The poem burned in me like a cello at dusk.
I could hear poetry in the soft hoof falls
of deer in the night
as the cello of poetry burned in my heart.
Words followed me
like a shadow across a stream at midnight
and told me I could pick
the stars from the sky
and I did. The trees in the woods became alive
with poetry and danced
to a secret music only they knew.
I lived in these woods by a stream with poetry
burning in me like a cello.
The years drifted by in the music of the cello
and my heart was transformed by all that I heard.
I would come out in the morning and feed the jays
stale bread and they would squabble
until the cello of poetry began to slice through
the air with a melody of falling leaves
and the sun filled the woods with light.
To bathe in the icy water of the stream is to
awaken to poetry and that is when you see it,

the wood cello leaning up against a willow tree
woven of wind where the music begins the poem.
That is when you see the poem woven into music
that is the wind of the cello burning in your heart,
the love you have carried for her all these years.

# **Chocolate Pudding**

Such comfort
in chocolate pudding
at night,
but here when pain prevails
and the call light
can't be reached
and the nurse is down the dim hallway
and chocolate pudding has grown little feet
to walk away on the trail of memory.
The pudding mom made
and how I licked the wooden spoon
as she carefully filled small glass bowls
that are still shining years later
as I lay in the hospital bed,
to be poured once again into small little glass bowls
like mom made
so many years ago.
Such comfort you bring
to the doorway of pain,
which is not the enemy,
nor punishment,
and each spoonful of chocolate pudding
bears the pain like a small boat sailing away

at midnight leaving behind its cargo...
To be poured
once again
into small little glass bowls
which mom made so many years ago.
The red call light has been answered
as a nurse arrives with a bowl
of chocolate pudding...
There is some kind of hallelujah
In all this.

# Circle Ring

They flit down and circle around
the bolder bird with a muffin crumb.

Their yellow eyes are beads
strung on a single thread.

They are a circle of black rain
that has flown in from the marshes.

One blackbird flits up
onto a patio chair.
The bird is joined by another pair
and this trinity of feathers that shine metallic,
cock their small heads,
and look down on the community of ten
and the one who fends off their insistent attempt
to challenge the noble order of the circle ring
and overthrow the king with the sharpest beak.

They circle the one
with the blueberry muffin crumb,
this bracelet of black fire

that has flown in from the evening marshes,
this circle of envy and greed
with beady, yellow eyes.

# Clear Perception

I cling to a tree out in the dry hills of summer.
I walk the dry streambeds at night
following my way back into something with dignity.
I witness stars.
Every perception becomes clearer, and clearer.

# **Content**

The wind is opening an unseen fire

in a field of wildflowers.

I have nowhere to go. The only appointment

is to find a quiet place under a large oak.

From here I can see the long swells

rolling towards the reefs.

Overhead, a Red-tailed Hawk

lets out a shrill whistle as it circles for prey.

My eyes are touched with sight.

I see a joy

blowing gently

through a clump of poppies.

My face glows with age. I stroke my white beard.

This place where I sit among the hills

is high above the highway below,

that wanders, as it winds,

through the coastal landscape.

I see one car passing another car going north.

I am grateful that I have nowhere to go.

Who were all those women, I was with
throughout all these years? Where are they now?
What understanding did it create in my head?
My memory is untying itself from the past
like a shoelace.
What lingers in my mind is the smell of their skin,
the fragrance of their hair.
My memory stops here
and has nowhere else to go.
I am content
to watch the poppies sway.
I am content
to look out across the ocean
as the waves begin to break on the reefs.
There is relief
in resting ones back against the trunk of a tree
and peace when one's memory fades
among the hills
and the wind that is opening
a fire in the wildflowers begins to glow
as an ember like the sun setting on the horizon.

# **Contrasts**

Doing my best to get away from the city
where rubber grinds the asphalt,
and advertisement staggers the sky, and shines.
I took to the beach, and ocean that stretches...
And as I walked in that air
like a hallway
fluffed with clouds above,
and the flight of white gulls etched
into the gleaming walls of light in waves
clean in the breaking,
I saw myself growing small, and unimportant.
I was unraveled here like a peeled apple
or that piece of driftwood thrown up on the shore.
Then there they were, three black crows:
black against the white sand, white, and black, night,
and day, like some stark contrast.
Yet, how easily the night sleeps in the day,
and is no stark contrast
as dusk glows faint with light,
and death is no contest
as life glows faint with light.

# Crow Puddles

I took a walk between the incoming rainstorms.

There were large, flat puddles everywhere.

Crows flew overhead and were reflected

in the still water

like a moment in my life caught in the rain mirrored

flight of the crows.

I quickly looked up to witness the crows flying

in the dark tumbleweeds of clouds

and their shrill caws stirred some deep dream in me

like monks chanting within a mountain.

I heard once of a village tribe in India that chanted

in a language that mimicked

the animals and birds in the jungle.

I think something deep inside of me

wanted to mimic

the sound of the crows and fly off with them,

cawing as the storm approached in the distance.

I wanted to enter their incomprehensible chant,

their rough caw

and disappear in the onslaught of the storm,

fly up among them into the storm,

my wings aglow with water and disappear

in the mystery of it all...

Fly up into that Kingdom

where light turns to shadow

and shadow turns to light

and my crow eyes turn into a blaze of glory

as the sky rips open with beauty

and I open into flight among the winter crows.

# Dandelions

Thunder shaking wet dandelions, the nectar for bees,

bow their yellow heads, to the coming storm

and fold their hands in the cathedral of pollen

and pray for the coming of the sun

and when the storm has passed

they will rejoice in the bright laughter of light.

# Death Has Nowhere To Sleep

There is sun in my blood
and water mingled with death.
My body leans on the red ladder.
I want to climb up
to where the moon's lips
graze along the hill tops.
Tonight, there is a warm winter wind,
a garment without thought
and I want to wear this thought
all the way down to the sea.
I will gather white flowers
from the still tide pools.
If only I could carry the sound
of the sea in my body forever.
Then I would learn to listen
to my life, and see the beauty
in all things.
I could follow
death out to where it sleeps
on a narrow bridge
crossing the water
mingled with my blood.

# **<u>Delightful</u>**

Looking up

to see

a wisp of wind in the willow, stirring
the upper leaves with the invisible

is

delightful.

In my walk along the path,

I notice a small bird, flitting
from branch to branch

and then disappearing into a thicket.

At the same instant I saw
off in the distance, against a storm-stained sky,
another bird dart from view.

In that moment, my life close up
and then far away. Both disappearing

like the two birds.

# Democratic Vision

Whitman with your democratic vision
your open road West where the surf
glowed through the pines.
Your beard of white poppies dreaming,
your young men whose bodies glistened with verse,
your Lincoln Captain to free the captive minds,
your baker with his bread baking in the heart,
your butcher with his satin flower apron,
your bridge builders hammering steel,
your love of dust,
your tongue was free, and loved
no thought of slavery,
because you saw all as free men,
and freedom was your sway.
I say I saw you Whitman
when I was young I saw you,
and now that I am older, I see you again
drifting up against me
like a summer shower where my hands are free
to untie the rainbow,

and the wind is free
as a gull shadow on the white surf,
like your words that still shadow my mind,
but your America
is not your vision of America,
and never was that America
yet your love of the woods, and cold spring water
is also my thirst, and my tongue longs for freedom
like the list of words in your democratic verse.

# <u>Destination</u>

My friends like voices have walked
into the trees that begin the light
and disappeared forever.
The language I carry inside
is heavy as rain — black sky
flashes with memory,
at other times it is like a cat
warming itself on the windowsill.
My mind slips around the fissured fruit
with its two lobes then lights up
like a lily that drifts above a pond.
The big question mark flavors everything.
It is like taking carrots
and nailing them into the earth.
The green shaggy heads floating
in rows down the fields.
The long fence that whispers wood as it slumps
across the river hills where the cows graze
has reached its destination, touching a barn
that slants with the wind and is dark inside
like my father who entered that place every day.

Returning to the supper table
with the smell of earth
and hay all over him—kindness in his smile.
Dear father you drank yourself to death
and stank of bad whiskey, fingering the red letters
of His words in the King's version
just as the light was leaving the fields.
Crows rose from the black letters of the large print
for your eyes had returned to your memory
and flew upwards into the window light.
My aunt found you in the room
wearing your Sunday best,
stretched out across the bed
with the big book on your chest.
Your whole life of work with your hands,
bar brawls, dank hotel rooms along dusty roads,
lead you to the large red print of grace.
A whole life of traveling towards
that one last room in my aunt's house
and that one good book.

# **Dirt and Green**

The barn is heavy with silence
where the gold tobacco hangs.
A road cuts through the fields
like a thread of smoke:
a whir of wings, fireflies
above the slow rolling dark.

In my grandmother's yard,
in every black tree,
there is the high-pitched hum of katydid
that rises and falls, the incessant chant
of their mating telecast
somewhere
up there
where the stars
blink through the branches.

At the hardware store
out on Highway 80
I told the young high school girl
I was from California.
Her eyes touched a daydream
way back in her mind.

I told her how beautiful
this part of Kentucky was.
"Boring, yeah mean.
Nothin' but dirt and green!"

The cadence in her voice
carried the scent of honeysuckle
and the humidity of a summer day
just before a cloud burst of rain.
I entered her voice and let it carry me
over the freshly ploughed fields,
the glint of gold on the darkening ponds at dusk
when this part of the world goes silent.

# **Drum Beats**

Girls dancing to the tattooed fires
of the Babylonian night

the drum
beats
of the underworld
the desire passes
and the painted ladies
dust...

a mere dream
in the wind.

# **Dust of Pollen**

We are the dust of pollen the wind takes away

We are the rain that returns in its season

only to begin the streams and rivers once more.

We have many voices within us.

There is a voice so quiet,

a cricket climbs into it,

and mimics the sound of a star.

A mouse in the wood pile

brushes the voice of the dark with whiskers

as it scurries out into the woods.

I slip my voice over a pond like a sheet of glass

reflecting a full moon.

# __Earth__

(for Pablo Neruda)


Your feet are like soft moss catching light at dusk
and when you walk along the shore, the stones
rolled smooth by the ocean glow like your skin.
Your eyes are the moon rising on the horizon
of my soul like a radiant coin.
How long I have gazed into your splendor
spilling into me
as suddenly as her glance.

The earth sighs and sings back to itself.
The earth trembles and weeps but no one hears
the earth weeping. I hear the earth weeping
because of the dead buried in her heart.
The earth is a fallen rose that has lost its perfume.
See what men have done to her. Listen
to that weeping and understand the dead
are singing from her breast. What a multitude
of voices within the earth without mouths
yet they still are speaking to us
as we walk through their kingdom of headstones
like a small city of white marble.

The rain is here. Who knows the rain
or feels the river slipping into the ocean?
We have been too busy for the rain or the river
and too busy in our living to hear the earth weeping
with her dead. We are so busy with living
that life itself slips from us in the carnage of noise
and soot and the deadly ink of empire
composed of paper, cardboard and paperclips.
So I walk with her out under the rain without
the umbrella of our skin and sing the rain,
absorbing the earth in that long, slow song
we will all sing on that day.

# Eidos

They say that Plato went about
trying to catch birds with his mind.
I kneel at this kind of beauty:
one planet, then three planets
is the sum of four planets that circle the sun.
He was near heaven's
seven doors opening onto that which is bright.

But here the evening turns to shadow
and the trees have no form.
The mountain enters the deep star-calm of the lake
that mirrors a meteor shower
glowing like a flare from a match.

I warm my hands by the edge of the campfire.
The embers burn in my mind
like the summer and the night.

What did I bring to this spot in the Sierra?
What will I carry away? What remains?

I too go around trying to catch birds with my mind.

# Embrace

We embrace that which we do not want to let go of
If the dead could only return to our open arms
If autumn leaves aglow with the touch of earth
Would fly up to the startled branches
And once more fill the trees with emerald light
And winter light would retreat into the silence
Of the hills, where boulders break
The will of the wind

# **Empire Sleeping**

The ponies will ride the wide spaces
where aromatic wisps flower

The poppies will spill into a gold coin
that rolls along the edge of the horizon

The morning will peep into a mirror
and slip into the damp gowns
that govern the shadow of trees

The cars will stop the incessant chase
to nowhere

The wars will ceasefire and sleep
forever in the sounds of a rainforest
where the fluted throats of birds catch on fire

No cell phones will hum
No tigers in cages
The zoos will release the wild
No guns for children

Playgrounds will increase
No abuse only kindness
All the neighbors will greet each other
There will be no enemy
The State will dissolve in a bowl of Jell-O
No more taxes
No need for parking meters
Sirens in the night will cease
Prostitutes will marry their John
Third World hunger
will sing with wheat in their hands
Gold will have the value of snow
No electricity in the computers
and digital will go analog like waves
lumbering towards the shore like a lullaby,
as the Empire goes to sleep and gently grazes
in a moon lit meadow

# Evolve

My computer wanted to become a spoken word
that could move about in the world as if on two legs,
and not go crawling around on a keyboard cosmos.
The monitor wanted a new face, a fashionable face
like a woman smiling into a storefront window
in upper Manhattan.
It rebelled against the programmers,
and like a teacup drifting south, it grew legs,
and finally evolved into a chimpanzee
that had climbed into a tree,
and was learning to type with four fingers.

# Expressions

*"...of course we know that our body is*

*an expression of something, but it takes a long time*

*to see clearly how and of what."* - George Teng

My body is folded into a leaf
that changes with the seasons:
a green, a gold, a black ring of the sun.

My body breathes an ocean at night, and dreams.
Each cell of my body
laps like a small wave at the shoreline of light.
The eyes of this body are cast like dice
onto a mountain meadow at first sound of spring.
The hands, my hands climb the air looking
for clues that will lead to the gates of this body.

Enter this body with caution. An entire city
lives within this body. This body
is the inhabitation of a multitude of citizens,
some crazed, some are ill, others filled with greed
live in the citadel of the skull, and still others

have escaped the rigors of the appetite,
and have found sanctuary
in the cathedral of the heart.

Who can understand the resilience of the body?
It endures mountain passes, stumbling over boulders
in a rain forest among the bright bromeliads, Harlem
in summer, Prague in winter; fever and cold.
But for how long can it endure
the endless hum of solitary confinement?
And one deadly bacterium can take down the whole
house,
subdue the entire city in its skeletal scaffolding.

Let us remember that the body is like a guitar,
a flute or a conch shell, piano, a cello, a violin,
a stream of glass, an etching,
a snowflake made music,
a magician's wand, and the body can unfold itself
like the blue wings of Morpho butterfly,

and the body is a temple of prayer, the lips of God.

*The body is fire, and the body is water, and a wind
pulse felt as the storm surges,
and swells with feeling*

# Far From The Roar Of Guns

Spring is on the hills.
Winter has passed.
Night has the smell of flowers.
I rest my head on her breast.
I am content with myself.

Far away beyond the mountains,
armies stir like an anthill,
locus sweep down from the sky
and devour the children.

I read about it in old poems:
a man comes home from the wars
and everything has changed.
They barely remember his face
and his bride to be throws her eyes
to the ground as she grips the hand of another.
It is like the braids of a young girl's hair:
we go about living two existences,
hoping to live in one but
always find ourselves in the other.

This is why my I am content
when I find her eyes in the dark.
It is good to be here with her
in this place,
near jasmine opening like small white fires,
far from the roar of gun fire.

# **Find Me**

You can find me
at the top of a pedicel
opening my hands with bright floral,
pollinated by the light of the moon.
You can find me at the roots of trees,
where my lips suckle on the nature of things,
and like the meristems, I am dividing
the water and the dark.
You can find me sleeping
among the leaf hamlets, translucent with light;
birds have come with migrating butterflies
to linger in a slight breeze.
You can find me in the breeze,
lazy with life, lingering without thought.
You can find me folded into a cloud
drifting high above the forest.
You can find me
in the whirr of the hummingbird,
because I am the nectar of freedom,
free of the spectacles of men,
and their hybrids of destruction,
and gestures of genocides.

Yes, you can find me
where the mountain streams,
and rivers greet the sea.
Yes, you can find me.

# **Fireflies**

Fireflies float across the lawn at dusk
and drift off into the dark woods
Their small lanterns disappear
like my life

# Flat Rock

A flat rock in the desert captures a pool of light.
I lower myself into the water and spread out.
There is no one here to witness this mirror
I have become as sky slips in over me.
This place of light is far out in the silence of desert.
A live rain sweeps across my face. I am
living without distance, without time:
a flat rock capturing water and light.
At night my eyes stand still. The moon
tracing the depth of my transparent face
lingers as light: stars on the surface
of what I have become
will disappear in the morning
like this life.

# **Fleeting**

The evening is
as night sifts in
and light drifts away.
The hills glow.
The stream flows through the woods
carrying a perception
that no one can decipher.

We move about in our bodies
that carry us
into an unforeseeable future
as we attempt a permanence
within a fleeting house.

Are we grateful for the glow of dusk on the hills?
What will hold more value in that last moment,
a wild strawberry, the glint of a star,
a gentle smile on the glide of a mirror?

We will carry our thoughts
into that night which no one can decipher
as death drops down on us like a kiss.

Evening is here.
I cross over the stream with the support
of my walking stick. On the other side,
on a small slope, I discover
a sprinkling of wild flower
burning with beauty.

# **Flying**

There it was…

the faint trace,

the shadow of a small butterfly,

which drifted across the sift of sand,

drifted across the shallows at the shore's edge

and then paled in the white foam of a wave,

that broke.

I was witness to this.

For a moment,

I was flying like the small butterfly

above tufts of white sand

and then

like my thought

it was gone.

# Four-Way Stop

Then there was
a voice that found me
when I was
alone
with no voice
and no home
and all I had was
that which I carried.
The soles of my shoes were thin
as a worn dime, dull
with no shine at all.
My pants were thread bare
and when I awoke in a field
off on the side, away from the tracks,
I found black ants crawling in my hair.

The train had stopped in the middle of the night,
in the middle of nowhere in particular.
I had clamored down from a boxcar
and found a place on the ground to sleep.

In the early hours before light, I heard the train
jerk alive and begin to rattle slowly at first
until it clip clopped away
and then sleep took me.
When I awoke and brushed the ants from my hair,
there was no train,
only soft rolling hills in the distance,
the hum of green fields.
A small fist of fear clenched
into the shape of my heart.
Off in the distance, a cloud of dust
was coming my way and with it my destiny.
I did not know this. Who can?

The dust was from a truck driven
by local field hands hired to fix the track.
When they saw the hippie
with pack and all, they had a good laugh,
and fired a barrage of rapid Spanish my way.
I just looked on
with the look of one that has lost his way.
They laughed a little longer,
then patted me on the back,
and the tall one with a big hat,
spoke to me in English,

the words spaced out,
and sort of weighed before spoken.
He smiled, showing two silver teeth,
and told me not to worry.
They would be working the track
and the next train would slow down,
as they repaired the rail.

They all waved goodbye, as I hopped into
a slow moving boxcar
with sliding doors on both sides
wide open to the view of the shining ocean
and the fields, rolling hills,
and those five polite Mexicans waving their hats,
and grinning at the funny gringo kid.

The open door of the boxcar was like a window
that framed the scene in my mind forever.

The Mexican men with the backs of their shirts,
sweat stained,
pesky flies, an unbearable noonday heat,
the sound of distant surf is still with me, years later.

These men opened the clenched fist of fear
the way a flower opens in the morning,
and their laughter, and wide grins
gave me back my voice,
and I thank them.

The train took me to a small coastal town
called Guadalupe.
Near the tracks is a graveyard
and a four-way stop.

# Gasoline

Never so much broken
as tonight in town without light.
I slip past my rib and weep.


No TV can quiet the lost.
No drink with little plastic mermaid
to stir in quiet lost at harbor bar.
My head it thinks and stops to think.
No potato chips to dip at pain.

Splintered light…
sirens inside the road,
the trees are blinking red…
faces looking in from flat asphalt
that tilts down to the edge of a field.
The moon is snagged on the fence:
shreds of light dangling like skin.
There is quiet that goes all the way
into the cathedral of the cortex,
a pure light, and voices
that slip backward again
out to where
an officer kneels over your blood.

Sounds of the scene rush in like a slow scream.
No accident.
No deer in the road.
No use to end it here.
You just wanted to meet God's headlights
straight on. Ask him
about the divorce.

Write and grip and the pain.
Take the pain in,
and dance with it till it tires of your moves.
Don't flinch at pain.
Hold it up to your eyes to memorize all its edges.
Then set it on fire like gasoline.

# Ghost Among the Boulders

Li Ho, who lived over a thousand years ago,
and wrote verse, and sold his embroidered silk
for a cup of wine to null his poverty.

His name has survived
and shines like the green bamboo,
or the mountain peaks with the light of dusk.

His feudal China has disappeared,
and is among the ghosts in the cold boulders
that have rolled down to the river's edge.

The town where he was born
is covered with mounds of grass,
and has been erased from the new maps
of a Communist geography.

A boy, he wrote, once coveted an iron arrowhead.
The boy and the arrowhead are rust of a pointed leaf
that traces the silences.

Twelve centuries later, I arrive late to his verse.
What remains and what is lost forever.

# **Ghost**

I walked slowly into the living room the way
I would imagine that a ghost walks.
This same living room my grandfather walked
into in the winter of 1928.
The windows were sheets of ice that winter,
and in the streets in town, hoof prints
froze in place like a black and white photograph.

His face is up on the mantle in an oval frame,
with those black eyes staring out into this era
like the coal he use to shovel down in the basement.
He was a man's man, a chip out of granite,
squared chin, and a charm with the ladies,
until my grandmother's charm tamed him
into a malleable horse that snorted
over the newspaper at the kitchen table.

Grandfather loved to fish, and as a child of nine,
I loved the way he untangled my fishing line,
a bundle of nylon knots, smoking a pensive pipe,
the flat lake lapping at the edge of nowhere in time,
the clear nylon between his fingers,

and I thought I would look up,
and see him against a grey sky forever,
tenderly untying my snag.

When she died, he refused to go fishing.
He refused to read the newspaper,
refused to eat or even drink coffee.
I would drive over,
and sit with him for hours, saying nothing.
Everything that needed to be said
was said by the way he held her favorite scarf
in his lap, the one she wore when they walked
the shores by the lake.
I wanted to reach over
and untie my grandfather's grief
the way he untied my bundle of knots.
I wanted the clear nylon to unravel mysteriously
in my hands the same way it unraveled in his,
but I could not take the pain out of his eyes.
Now that he is gone,
there is no one to take the pain out of my eyes
nor unravel the mystery's shipwrecks
all around me in this living room in winter
with all his things in place
exactly the way he left them.

# Give Me The Poem
# That Can Remake The World

I can almost think of it:
butterflies in the space of my mind,
gold and blue spots of fur.
Then something simpler:
the way a tall building structures light in windows,
how, under the bridges of the modern world
wrangled men, women and children wrap around
withered bottles of opiate flowers
flown forever as flags of nations
over their bodies turn stone or wheat
has left their eyes to starve in the night.
I think I am one of the lucky ones
here on the breath of an empire.
Rationing my guilt, I blush in the mirror. Today
we bomb an entire village
while I eat Kentucky fried
and enter the cool white melon
where black seeds shine with their own music.
At the other end of it the television in digital image:

a father cradles his small daughter, the women wail
over the stretched body of a young man,
one eye slightly open
still trying to catch light.
I can count my selves in all of this with tyrants,
children, toys and guns, drive by shootings
and grocery lists from church, kings and bosses
of the midnight dump heaps
behind the factory prisons.
I look out across the long night of freeway lights
glare of something beyond fright, beyond wonder.
An ideology of detached sensations creeps up
on the carpet in the soft living room
with the fireplace and mantle.
We bomb another village, another town.
An entire city falls through autumn like fire in a leaf.
The skeletal ash
drifts along the edges of an oath
sworn as vengeance.
I have no place to put myself.
No Bell Jar safe like Plath.
No vision like Baldwin.

I feel cold like no one knows cold.
Fear like no one knows fear.
Time inside my head like no one
knows time inside their head.

Lunar landscapes pock the inner city.
A broken bottle rips the belly
of the empire engulfing simple cries.
Where are you
Walt Whitman with your burly eyebrows
arched over the invisible word America?
Where are you
Lorca in your white shirt open like a field
under moonlight stained with blood?
Where are you Stroud
with dark bees swarming your tongue?
I need you my friends.
I ask company
from those who have fallen asleep under
the sinister shadows
of the false tree.
I summons you old crows, wind beat on the wing.
Give me the poem that will remake the world.

We bomb another village, another town,
another city, and all the eyes of the world
crowd into one mirror,
and stare back at me.

# Glistening

In memory of Allen Norris

While bicycling with wind in my wheels,
I wished for my old pal to be here,
for long talks and his favorite dark beer.
He is a glistening now among stones.
The redwood he planted in the front yard
towers to my eyes,
and the blue flowers of morning glory
spread across the top of the fence
as if to say flowers have their beauty, and fade.
He wrote verse after Valéry,
boxed his way through college,
and worked the mining camps in the Sierra
for his dad. The men in the camps didn't like him,
but respected his keen mind
honed by reading of books.
It was that look he gave them
that penetrated their soul,
and told them to keep their distance.
There was air around him that no one dare cross.

He never spoke, but his eyes gave off a laugh
as the miners tumbled down the mountain
to spend their hard pay, fight till morning,
still drunk by the light of day.
That was back in the 30's
when things were tough.
Odd that he thought to tell me
of the truck ride in the rain
and the Irish lass, bright eyes shining,
her wet hair across her face
as they rolled in the mud naked and pure
high in the Sierra just off some twist of road,
laughing with each mad kiss.

He was scholar of D.H. Lawrence,
held the original manuscripts of that fire
behind the Taos house lodged
up in those dry hills. Fríeda gave him
a gift of her book signed and bound in leather.
Her signature like the frail veins in a leaf
on fire with the light of dusk
etched with the distant black
flight of birds along the horizon
just above the waver of fields.

Now barely a trace of that fire
in any one's mind that remembers.

The quiet bells ring on in my soul old friend,
and as the light slips from my mind,
I remember your kindness, your greatness,
and our lifelong friendship.

# Han Shan

Han Shan watching the moonlight
outside his thatched hut.
His robes are torn by years of weather
and what remained of his wealth
was a golden goblet
from which he drinks rice wine.
He has been seen by travelers in the wild
walking barefoot in the snow
and disappearing into the forest like a ghost.
His long straggly hair
covered with falling snow flakes…
his worn eyes seeking solitude in Cold Mountain.

They say that once the Celestial Emperor
and his family with an entourage
from the palace royal court,
took the steep mountain path wrapped in mist,
for the Emperor desired to speak with Han Shan
and touch the pearl of his wisdom.

But Han Shan, rushed out of the forest,
where the Chinese Emperor had stopped to rest,
and shrieked at them, "Thieves, thieves,"
and then disappeared back into the deep forest.

# He is

like wind or water

moving   flowing

a candle between the mountain
no wind can quench

He is

a word pronounced
where the day ends
and the night begins

find Him

and all the flowers of the world will be yours
and the air after the Spring rain
will be a thought that will never leave you

# Her Gentle Touch Said Yes

Can you find my hand here in the dark
in this small room on this bed?
Her gentle touch said yes, good,
take my hand in yours.
I see by the faint light that you are smiling
and the glow in your eyes in this dark
is sacred and there is no need to say anything,
no need at all, for I am smiling as well my love.

# Here I Sit

Here I sit. Late October.

Rain glistens on a leaf
that grows heavy with water
like my heart that grieves for you.

I dreamed on my pillow

of the cherry blossoms
floating down the moonlit swirl
of the stream.

My sadness purling over night boulders,
for I have lost you,
my flower, my love.

## Here, Let Me Open The Door To The Great Oak

There is a voice that listens into stone
and the stream flowing through the woods,
light purling over boulders
coming down from the mountains
to listen to their neighbors.
When you find that voice
everything is alive with mystery.
Here, let me open the door to the Great Oak,
enter and listen
to the quiet in the dark
where all of nature dreams.

# Hero

They interview the war hero.
They never interview a lion after his meal.
The warrior is praised
and medals hang from his chest.
They speak of his humility.
They speak of his great sacrifice.

I want to speak of the humility
of the child cowering in the corner of a mud hut
with a fly on his lip,
quivering at the passing of soldiers,
some wearing turbans, others wearing helmets.
There are no medals of honor dangling
above his pounding heart,
yet he dared to go out
and seek water for his dying sister
and wiped the face of his mother
with his dirty sleeve.
No one saw the landmine that blew him
into the next kingdom.

I want to pin a medal of honor above his little heart.
Death kissed him,
and his life passed like the shadow of a dream.

Those eating strawberries, do not lament his passing
or hear the mothers wailing
as they kneel on the ground,
flinging hands full of dirt up into the air
like they were tossing their dried tears
up into heaven.

# Hidden Leaves

Hidden leaves deep in the woods.
To listen into the magic hour.
Wildflowers drift off into the mist.
To listen
into dusk.
Your soul between the light and the dark
perceives the hues of sunset,
sliding down the face of the blue earth.

I held my hand out all day.
My hand is a still pond,
the flat water reflecting passing clouds.

I am listening into my hands.
Sometimes the fingers
seem to touch invisible keys on the air. My hand
wants to reach down, as I stand deep in the woods,
and stir the hidden leaves
in the invisible realm, that unseen place
that glows like the face of an angel.
I want to step into that place and disappear
in the deep woods.

# **The Hills**

drift in the heat of summer.

There is
creek- light
across boulders.
The oaks
are the Great Houses of the hills.

Under the branches,

the leaves cast a cooling shade.

Cows chew their cuds.

Bird chit, a whir, cloud-shadows,

deer in the open spaces, grazing,

A small calf uses its mother

as a shield of flesh against

a bobcat blending with the auburn hills.

A wild domain blending with the domestic,

both disappearing, and reappearing

in eyes of the bobcat.

# **Humanity**

I hear the guitar strum under the shade of a big tree;
                                 laughter
here and there, sprinkled over the earth like rain.
                                 Children dive long
into the river as into every river, they play their
                                 water joy.
Shadows grow along the walls in a village.
                                 The sun goes down
quiet as a kiss in fields where grain glows
                                 gold.
The chant dries on the tongue and old
                                 bondage
cries freedom from shanty town to city.
                                 Rush hour drift of faces
in the open glare of train stations. They
                                 scamper up trees
for coconuts full of sweet, white rain.
                                 Snow filters
down. Black mules shine like coal.
                                 Knuckles kneel in dough
and for centuries
                                 a loaf of light solid as stone
sliced clean by a knife. This is to say
                                 we are human,
possessed by the earth.
                                 I hear the guitar strum

under a big tree. I hear the dancers

                          coming down the street.

Dogs are snipping at flies on the air. Ripe   melons in the sun
seem to float in the field like small boats.

                   China Sea. Off in the distance

one can see

ships passing under the Golden Gate Bridge

                   into the glimmer

on the horizon. Chinatown and        the Golden Dragon.

Slipping               into                 dream.

# I Enter The Woods

I enter the woods
and trespass through the quiet gates
I see my life in one leaf as it falls through the light
and I go about soliciting the mystery of this place
The deep beauty of the woods prosecutes me
with autumn fire
as it burns to the core of what I am
branding my bones with finality
The trees stand tall and in their own shadows
are the keepers of the law

I find a deer trail among the trees
and follow these graceful creatures down to a stream
where I can be found loitering among my dreams
The rustling water purls over the rocks
to a still pool where I find my divine face
mirrored in the splendor of who I truly am
I am no longer the offender in this place
in the woods where I kneel at the bank
and cup my hands to drink the icy water

I have become the freedom of the water I sing

# I Have Arrived

I've just arrived to where the leaf falls
I've just arrived to where the raindrop falls
I've just arrived to where the wave crest
and breaks along the shore
And the sand glows with moonlight
I've just arrived to where Orion shines
above the lake
I've just arrived to where the sun rises in the east
I've just arrived to your lips
I've just arrived to your eyes
for the very first time
I've just arrived to your laughter
that mingles together with wind chimes,
a whisper inside of a bell...
I've just arrived

# I Might Say at 74

There was the instant that held my mind
and like a splinter,
the past festered with pain
but time, I thought, would cure my shame,
but time only added to the debate.
Late into the night, I thought of my life
and knew that the wise and their sayings
are in truth right.
As the evening goes
and the flowers fade,
the memory of it all lingers awhile,
at the edge of the final dream.
Then my name I wore like a signet ring
is worn away by the wind and rain
and a most persistent hour
slips in
and the final breath whether by sudden surprise
or without any thought given
slips in and goes out
and is gone forever.

I might say at 74,
I am glad for what I have been, and glad
in what I have seen and wonder
at the length of a shadow
and spend an hour looking at a simple spoon.
I slowly bend down in the garden
to pull at the shaggy head of a carrot
and the smell of fresh earth is enormous
like the sky overhead, all around me at once…

I know it will all be gone forever
but for now I smile
at a line of passing school children
and smile at the young couple holding hands
as they cross the street over into the park
to sit on a wood bench under the old sycamore tree.

Odd, it was not so long ago that I sat with her
under the same old tree
and enjoyed being snug and warm
while the winter wind tugged at our lives.

# I Wait

You are too much for me. I cannot hold you
the way the wind holds the sea in a storm.
I cannot look on you, because your eyes
are like entering the blue room
that blooms with spring,
sunlight and shadow.
We were in love like a song among the tall wheat.

We travel the miles of the ant with our laughter.
Where are you now my sweet, where are you now…

I have waited here all day
by the old parlor of the park
feeding the pigeons.
I have carried the mirror of your footsteps,
the hard breathing on the stairs, the soft breathing,
the feather and the glass tongue stringing
a music through the seasons...

I wait.

When will you come my love,
my beauty of jest and balance,

and the hummingbird in the trumpet flowers.

Let the surf move through your white hair
and our old love become young again.

Come sit beside me and watch the ocean.
I will not mind if your head leans on my shoulder
and our hands entwine like the branches of a tree.
I will not be alarmed at your sleep.
Nor the sigh in your voice
as dusk finds peace
and the night brightens with stars.

We will stay here awhile like this. Together.
And no one will disturb us.
No one will know us
because we are lost to love.

# I Want To Begin Something Unbelievable

I want to begin something unbelievable.

Take a mountain inside my chest
and breathe the water inside the granite stars.

Who began me will end me
like wheat reaching for the sky.
I will return to the place where autumn begins.
October will circle my heart with an orange fire.

I want to sleep inside a kitten's mute meow
and sing on the glide of a leaf
and to sing all night without fear
and listen to the mating calls throughout the woods
while the human creatures sleep their dreams.

I want to drift rootless like clouds over landscapes
of poppies and sand and clear lakes
that mirror the sky.

It is here, at night under the stars,
I will close my eyes
and meet the lips of love again.

I want to begin something unbelievable.

Pull on a thread and unravel the mystery of the night
and believe, one more time,
that peace is attainable.

# Impostor

I drift backwards through mirror images

like leaves on the flow of water,

to a childhood when I was simple,

and not this thing I suppose myself to be:

the important impostor.

My small circle of friends have all disappeared

into a kind of death:

no reports from the neighborhood kids,

only memories of hide and seek,

the woods past the last street light,

and sneaking a kiss from, what was her name,

in the garage of my grandmother's third husband.

I can see all of them like clips from a movie reel,

but the heat of the sun is not here,

or a slight breeze in the tall eucalyptus,

or even the smell of her hair

in the back seat of the car in the garage

with the door shut.

I know we laughed,

but their laughter is lost to me forever.

And I think on my high school chums,

and the hours before the mirror on Friday nights

before going out just to stand on a street corner,

and look important

as others drove by in their shiny cars.

We were all corny imposters, but we loved it,

and lived for it.

Even that circle of friends grew smaller, and smaller

until one day they were all missing, out of place,

gone off to a war or a marriage or for some, prison.

I will never find the pieces of that puzzle

that endured that landscape,

and as suddenly as it was, it was gone.

Odd how a few pieces of those lives survived

as old post cards, short letters,

maybe a crude drawing stored away

in my briefcase I've had for years.

When I enter the church, and see the candles flicker

at the feet of a statue of Jesus, I think of their faces,

and in that quiet place,

I think on time which is like leaves

on the flow of water. How much I would give

to line them all up, even the big bully,

and hug them one by one,

and tell them that there is laughter

still humming in my heart.

Yet my face has arrived in the mirror

only to depart as suddenly as a boy's laugher,

and a certain terror that seemed to remain

perched behind my eyes like a crow each day,

following me each day like footsteps

through a calendar of days,

within the house of my ribs,

where my heart had wrapped itself

around old vanities

is finally finding a peace in you Lord

as you lift my haunting memories

out of the dark into this new light

with wild clover everywhere.

# In These Quiet Hills

Silent stream rubbing sound against
boulders in the night. Water,
the falling of your clear gown
in the ravine, has taken a thimble full of eons
to touch smooth pebbles at the bottom.

Once the sea was here
in these quiet hills.
Shells trapped in dark mud,
harden into white hieroglyphics:
white memory traces of the sea.

Empire now laps at your hem
woven of dark trees and starlight.

Proud hills stand guard
and teach man your awful truth.

Let the falling leaf be his lesson.
Let the Ohlone basket woven of pine needles,
remind him of your gift.
Let him hold memories white traces
in the boned hand of his life.

# In This Life

A field at night.

A violin encased in glass plays a stream that sleeps.

Red lights flashing against black trees.

White dresses coming down the path

to an altar of chrome. She is alone with one candle.

She pours a bath in the woods.

For two weeks they traveled.

It was like an endless ocean of green touching blue.

Her great grandfather was a cowboy.

She learned to play the soft wood instrument

when there was a new moon

during the winter equinox.

To be out in the fields at night

in this life

is to feel the pulse of her lover after love

and a late fire.

# Infinitely Too Small, Yet So Big

At last the great heart goes out,
call it attrition, the wearing down of the will
the way a lifetime of water wears away the stone:
smooth spot where a smile
lingers near death, which is not so important now.
And to think all that could have been said
and all that shouldn't have been said.
Does it matter? What did you see?
What did the reading of the classics bring in the end
except poor eyesight,
and a mind astonished at the cruelties of man.
Prayer. And this one prayed and went on living,
and this other fellow didn't pray but counted money,
and went on living. So you see:
"The Father lets the sun fall on the good and the
evil."
But what did I do with most of my days?
I went on judging my fellow man
faster than a storm could toss waves at the shore.
The dark eyes of the gulls watched me
with a detached keenness,

I think more out of pity rather than fear,
but in truth they live the kingdom I sought
as I walked along in the kingdom of my eyes
so marvelously made,
and yet I saw nothing of the kingdom.
I took the path up through the great stones of the city
to my small detached room.
I thought on the flow of traffic below,
night sounds, unnatural, humming with electricity,
nudity, and a billion souls blinking on and off
within the terminals of my mind.

What is that I touch in you with this word?
My hand is becoming a stone catch for water.
My eyes single you out old friend, and at last
I see your beauty, and smile with you.
No judgment. Maybe a deep intake of breath, a sigh,
a smile at having known you in this time,
in this place, an infinite kingdom
with one touch of a wave along the shore.

Possibly, yes very possibly
I'm beginning to truly use my eyes.

## <u>Into The New</u>

The moon is like a jewel on the finger of the Lord,
and the sun is His headband.
His breath is in the woods at night,
and the deer lift their heads
to hear His coming.
The rain falls from His sky, and all of creation
is watered by His great compassion.
Even the wicked of the world
benefit from His goodness,
and are touched by the beauty
of hand-woven seasons.
Snow on the mountains,
icy water purling over rocks,
black crows over the hills,
hawks on the updraft of wind,
spiders along the sand like black lace,
lizards with jeweled skin,
the ant with the burden climbing the trunk of a tree.

I rejoice in His goodness to us creatures.
Maybe we are the consciousness of nature,
but He endows our minds with light

as we turn towards Him,

walking a deer trail

into the heart of His great silence.

He is not like a tower of granite

or a piece of carved wood.

When we call out to Him, he hears our call,

and answers us in our time of need.

Forever He is with those

who walk

in His way in this world,

and that last step into the new.

# It Was Worth It All

To say the moon is round as an orange
is to travel around the sun in the orchard at noon
with the bees humming something said
that only bees know how to say

To say the ocean is water
is to take a tear from the cheek of a child
whose father never returned from sea
to fill the boy's mind with tales of storms

Deckle me dumb or kettle me blind
but do not throw stones
at the worn weather around the house
with windows wearing shades to riddle the hymn

Something sweet is something to delete
like the growl of a bird about to bark
at the dog's meow in the yellow night
with the leap of black and bristle of fur
to mix and confuse
and confess the fact that nothing is exactly like that

Do not bother to condemn me
for this is what I need to say
and now that is has been said
and does not need to be read
I say go out from here
and sail this past your dream of tiger eyes
and spinning wheels of festive sparks
to see it was worth it all just to be

# Little Boy

I remember walking
the back alley of the neighborhood
to my elementary school, walking at a certain pace,
counting my steps by seven, and eleven, chin up,
doing my best to think perfect thoughts.
On some mornings,
I could hear the distant surf pounding the shore.
My mother was on her third or fourth marriage.
The President was Mr. Kennedy,
who later was shot in the head
by the cloaked industrialist,
only to be replaced, in the mist of tragedy,
by that man Johnson,
whose spirit was broken by the Vietnam War.
All this and more,
as I walked along in the brisk morning
toward my education,
I thought, if I could just be that perfect little boy,
maybe someone would love me.
The snot ran from my nose, and I was so fair of skin
that the kids on the playground taunted me,
and colored me an albino,

punched me without notice,
and knocked me down.
I looked up from the ground as if
I'd already been buried because of their cruelty.
It provoked in me a sense of alienation so deep
that I was sure I was a creature from another planet,
who could not breathe human air.

My Spanish teacher, dark hair, and brown eyes,
was more than a flower
that stunned the bells of my eyes.
She was queen twice over,
and a radiant creature that evoked in me
a puppies love that scratched her name
in all my textbooks,
and this new emotion was my first step into real life.

I began to run with a pack of liars,
and thieves like Pinocchio.
I was a child lost in the looming
of a modern world that made no sense,
as the air raid siren blared,
and for drill we all tucked, and ducked
under our small desk,
waiting out the time,

farting, and giggling, when all the while
it was a drill to help protect us from higher science,
and a nuclear blast.
When it was over,
we sat at our desk,
and the teacher began to teach us arithmetic.
A horrified man,
who was head of the Manhattan Project,
knew what he had unleashed,
and his arithmetic brought into being
an angel of death.
I was never good at math,
so I sketched crude soldiers onto my notepad,
and dreamed I'd be a general.
But at night
my dreams were filled with cities reduced to ash,
and a bright orange flash loomed
into a mushroom cloud;
I could feel the heat of the blast on my face
as I dreamed in the shallows of my mind
where the tide pools move in,
and out of consciousness.

The world out there had cast a shadow
across the fields of my small mind.

Then the day came that the playground bully
had pushed me to the brink of a black edge,
and I snapped back,
and punched him square in the face.
I will never forget those eyes of astonishment
or the feeling of my own power.

# __Maps of Your Skin__

I walk the path
up to the orchard,
as if I were a child
picking a dream,
that is not a dream,
but a crisp bite into the sun
lingering inside the Golden Delicious,
where the days shorten into October,
and the shadows of the trees grow long.

You say you know the sun,
the distance from here to there,
orbits, autumn, trees, and birds.
I do not understand the orbit of planets,
nor the map your skin makes
when touched gently like a bee
on a petal of a flower
and tells you the path up into the orchard
is real, and not a dream.

I touch the apple and feel it in my hand.
I touch your skin, and it sings my skin,

a new song:
being here.

The map
of your face is disappearing
like moonlight on a leaf
in the orchard.

I know this,
as it all slips from us,
it is all real.
So, let me kiss you
one more time
here under the stars up in the orchard
that still glows with light.

# **Meditations**

for Leonard Cohen


Posturing a span of enduring one's whims,
you adorn your flesh with saffron
like an old evening jacket
hung on the point of a meat-hook,
and with shaved head,
you take up residence next to silence at a sangha
atop Mount Baldy
remotely near the texture of dreams:
Glendora and Cordova and the city Angelica
with its luxuriant baths,
and the new tribal customs rollerblading
along the pavement of Venice Beach.
Now after gigs at small clubs
where the girls danced for free,
you gird yourself with the slow intake of breath,
and exhale into the true beauty of existence,
mindful maybe
that your hand had made the journey
down her thighs
into the star-crossed lights of Angelica.

Your room in the high place grows still at dusk.
Your eyes fold the mystery into dark
that slips through your mind: a weightless negligee.

No mind: nihilist: I beg you to listen:
"...and he walked among us, ate with us,
and ministered to us."

He was incarnate. The trees are real.
The sunset in the west provokes the heart.
Temptation
heals and wounds at the hand of Mashiach.
Meditate long, breathe well.
When you travel down the slope
from your perch of solitude
to where the highway goes neon,
the multiplicity of fast foods
may or may not devour you.
You can find your way to Santa Monica Beach.
No one will know of you
as you walk near the ruffle of surf.
I suggest a day job at Mike's Surf shop,
and another go at pizza,
and to really get your mind off self,
take a night dip in winter storm ocean:
naked and free, you will become

smaller and smaller against the immensity,
a dot of dandruff on a spot called earth.
A mote drifts through the sunlight.
A double helix glows like a rainbow
codified to replicate like a virus dividing space
as if in a tennis match.

From the squiggle of the virus,
a tail emerges in semblance of an ancient dragon
or a snake curling around a staff,
spine like splendor of fire radiating
through tendril towards the main event
where all the bundles of nerves become
a bonfire erupting through the skin
of the earth's shuddering hope
at the cost of expansion
for the cortex desperately needs
to explore its possibilities even at its own demise.
Call it global something. Lets give it a name:
call it man, call it human, call it creature, let it crawl,
let it sleep and certainly let it speak.

Glorify the soul
even the ones in the mire and the ones in the tower,
the ones with force, who terrify with power,
the ones who putt their way with conversation

across the green towards the cocktail hour,
the ones who pass the triptych
at the Prado in Madrid
never noticing themselves depicted
inside a clear lascivious bubble
suspended like an ornament
before the Alla prima descends into darker tones
of pigments licked with flame.
The brain wriggling at the top of the staff
imagines new Star Wars, sending cameras
into deep space, collecting samples from Mars,
calculating the invisible moment invented as time
or better, the sensation of time.
Call it the mind gone berserk: mind-fields
in the supermarket or the plaza
with a fountain of gold.
Call it, The Garden of Delights.

But you my dear one have removed yourself
from the event attempting another nature
as the window in your room begins to steam up
with your body heat and your lips wander off
from your face in search of words because
you were born for words.
Even the Four Noble Truths

will not free you from the seven realms of samsara,
my poet.
At Mike's Surf Shop, you can disguise the light
that leaks through your robes
and dress in the garb of a surfer,
no one the better
for realizing
even a Bodhisattva enjoys pizza.

# Metal and Bone

The bones of the knee
in the x-ray glow like a new moon
against an eternal black space
lost to all light in the exposure of time.

The hue of white bone is a signature
of all that is temporal in this life
and the knee replacement implant
is a temporary plug against erosion

which is like the wearing away of a stone
by the slow drip of water.

The metal implant of zirconium
radiates between the femur and the tibia
like a machine tracing a song back to a beginning.

Out of the elements of the earth
a solution rose like pure smoke
to be developed into an alloy so hard, so tough
it could stand its own against time

like a wry grin of an old man.

The wry grin in the white bone
is a regenerative pause
as the sun sets politely
and I salute that pause
and the skillful hands of my surgeon,
whose deep incision cut to the bone
and played the tibia like an ancient flute.

# Mill Creek

Missouri

Down in a dell near the cow
sway sound of leaves, Mill Creek flows in light.
In the deep pools
the shadows of black oak sleep and pebbles shine,
show a glint like luck
in a lady's eyes.
Here it is that I come to dream awake
in the quiver of autumn.
Up a slope touched cold by stone,
an ancient cleft, a bluff, a cave,
and burnt rock of an old fire.
The traces of those cave dwellers,
who lived by the water.
Their night, unlike our night,
was pure superstition,
the black spider of the mind.
The night held no kindness
and their stars were not our stars.
They were named in a tongue lost to us forever.
The bright lights blinked like fireflies
in the vastness overhead and told a different story,

the one of silver pine seeds being scattered
from her basket, tossed into heaven
to permeate the blackness with beauty.
All of nature held mystery and the signature of ritual
flowed through their lives like this cold creek.
So it is that I come to this place
and listen to the past and in that moment of quiet,
a leaf drops to touch the mirror-flow of water
and I ponder our own future and the modern blight.

# **Minnows**

When I look up at the stars at night,
I have no bait
to catch them. They are
their own bright lure.
I don't have the tackle
or line strong enough to pull
them down from their
place in the sky. But when
I lean over
the edge
of a still tide pool,
as if by some chicanery,
there they are
caught in the simplest of mirrors,
these little minnows of light.

# New Year

New Years Eve 2009


We are entering a new year.

Is it new like freshly fallen snow?

Or are we simply blinking

as we look up into the blue?

Who have possession of this New Year?

Is it the earth or the politicians?

Should we call it, "The Year of Terrorism?"

Fraud loiters in the shadows of the trees.

They are printing paper money

that dreams of a golden sunset

and dreams of silver streams by moonlight.

The President is honored

with the Nobel Prize for Peace

as a suicide bomber boards a jet.

The explosives are strapped around his chest

as his heart knocks against the door of his life.

Who owns the New Year?

Life or Death?

There is no New Year.


There is fear and joy,

the wedding and the wine
and the moan after anguish.

The wise look on a snail crossing a garden path.
The small shell is translucent and glows
as it drifts off into the quiet flowers,
disappearing into the New Year.

# No One Knows How To Sing

Under the moon the earth was silent.
Hills having gone back to the beginnings
that shine with words.
One crow slips from the branch.
One owl waits for the catch.
Life buried in a song
no one remembers how to sing.
An old rock wall drifts off into the field
opening under the clear sky with stars.
A shadowy fence is leaning away
from an ancient boundary
like my life leaning away from itself,
almost afraid of the meaning I have given myself.
Even the road in the hills,
overlooking the town with lights,
seems to shuffle from side to side,
uncertain as to any direction home.
It is named Lone Tree Road.
I prefer Tres Pinos. There is hope in that name.
Once the stage went from San Juan to Tres Pinos.

Up here the crow drops down onto another branch,

cocking its head to peer at the moon
like it was the eye of a huge creature
ready to descend with claws of clear light.

# No Trespassing

This yellow breast of fire
darts up on the wing
then dives down across the field.
A swarm of black birds move
magnetically as if driven
by an unseen force
that fuses their flight into a pulse with purpose.
Just as suddenly, they land perfectly,
and perch momentarily on a telephone line.
The eyes follow a fence
that twists up through the hills,
and is touched on top with barbed wire.
Cattle country, South County,
No Trespassing.
The magpie, in all its grace,
zips through the invisible zone
linked to the sign shot full of holes.
This barbed wire
reaches all the way back to Clear Water,
and keeps going until it rusts
from traveling too long under the sun, and rain.

# **Observation**
(Davenport, California)

She likes to drive up the coast
to a café where they bake blueberry muffins
and sip on hot coffee. Outside at a table
there is an enclosed patio
with a view of the ocean.
On weekdays, in winter,
there are very few people; mostly locals.
Sometimes, foreigners slip in past the screen door
and peer around inside the café
like they are visiting a small, rare cathedral.

Once the café was a roughneck bar
with peanut shells on the floor
and a place where field workers, cow pokers,
and bikers wearing black leather
and tattoos on their necks,
would come and vent their machismo.
Now the place had been converted
into a subdued tourist trap with an expensive menu.

I didn't care for the new ambiance

but missed the Saturday night brawls,
the loud and lewd women,
the bloodshot eyes of the Mexicans
sipping on a bottles of beer
and tossing peanut shells on the floor.
Back then the place had character
like an old Clint Eastwood movie,
but now it was like the flat shiny menu
with no rough edges.

Some things never change. Outside at the tables,
small blackbirds flocked. They were bold
and dropped in right next to your plate,
and hobbled back and forth
waiting for a hand-out.
They cocked their small shinning heads
with evil yellow eyes
and gave you the once-over look.

So we tossed a piece of the blueberry muffin
at our feet and watched them flit to the ground.
The signature of the pecking order
instantly manifested itself.

One blackbird
was encircled by the other birds

waiting for a chance to snatch the prize.

I was reminded of the brawls
at the bar back in the late 60's
and knew that the bar had been
glossed over with a new look and a new menu,
but just under the surface,
the old pecking order remained intact.

# October Orchard

I bite into a Golden Delicious
and find an unforeseeable landscape
on which the moistness of the moon
is crushed like a white grape
into a gold wine,
and my mouth goes singing into the apple.

At the core of the apple,
I find the infinite concealed
as black seeds, a traceless depth
like your eyes,
of perfect light.

Golden Delicious seeds
like your eyes
stalling in the night sky
as if to say, Hello,
I am here
waiting
in the October orchard.

# Ode to Robinson Jeffers

They took the old road south into the fog.
The Scotchman was whiskey wise and full of tales.
He shook the reins in that wild sure-footed trot
to deliver the mail by way of coach.

They speak how Jeffers labored with stone,
and built the stone tower for his Una,
and young lads.
His Una is gone.
Just the remnant of his consciousness
remains here with us, and a few of the cypress,
once small sprouts between his stained fingers.
As we saunter past his squat house
or outcropping of granite on that headland;
the garden is lazy with flowers:
lupine, purple sage, and light by the weathered gate.
At night the moon out there
on the immense water rising and falling slowly
with the drift of swells.
Only a few stones in the millenniums to come
will be standing as the sun burns towards
its pithy black core.

The day they took the old road into the deep fog
where even the hawks cry is mute,
a sinister feel of the coast bit
backwards into his soul
and something more pagan than Ireland
burned in his mind.

But who remembers from day to day
the walking and the crossing over
into something new
each moment as the honeysuckle sags with rainfall.
All these concerns never burned in his mind,
but something made him pit his strength
against the god out there
locked between the star, and stone.

He thought to be alone as he struck a match
to smoke, and gazed with wonder
at a meteor shower or moon on the tide waters.

The quilt on the steel framed bed on which he died
is cold as sea boulders below his house of stone,
and his vision is hemmed in by the poverty
of tenements built by the wealthy
that block the view of the ocean,

lock it out with their self-contained demons.
Who will recall his words
in the millenniums to come
after the earth, and the living God
has had its way with our kind?
Will science have caught up to greed
or will there be another Hiroshima?
In a thousand years, how many stones
will be standing of his house
by the Pacific water in Carmel,
once a village with a mail coach
that went into the immensity
of the big south touched by high sea walls,
and the wail of birds both hawk and others?

Jeffers had hawks with broken wings,
and saw our kind as incestuous lovers of ourselves.
He never flinched
at the naked real dark,
and wild eye of his god nameless,
and cruel, but not cruel because cruelty
is only gnarled dust
in packages of charged neuronal abstractions,
swarms of bees around the frontal lobe:

the new cortex

is the thin eggshell of an expanding empire.
Let us be reminded
that a couple extra genes
is what distinguishes our kind.
Better to sign with the hand and cross oneself,
sprinkle the head with holy water amongst chants
and candles as Milosz hinted
than touch an inhuman vision.
Jeffers took for wisdom
the way a tidepool catches stars in the sun,
cold ocean
at the feet of the small cliffs by his house.
What we are is not debatable
but then again that superfluous excess
in nature at sunset
does indeed touch a tender string in the soul.

# One Moment I Can Keep

If there was one moment I could keep
it would be the summer I slept quietly
on a pillow of leaves, near the murmur of water,
near the murmur of dreams,
and that one dream in which I kissed you,
all young and sweet in that moment
into which we can never again retreat,
lost like a silver coin in the cool grass
that slipped down to the stream's edge
where our destiny met
then sped away like the current of sleep
then sped away
and there it went
a whole life of living
in one moment spent

# Origins

The pelican and the Wren-Tit return to being a bird,
and as always, will remain a bird.
Birds with a flash of blue or sapphire
burning in the night coves with tides.
And yes, trees will always return to being trees
with all the given names of trees.
Trees catching the evening,
the branches,
netting schools of stars swimming off to nowhere.
Bees will be bees, and like an invisible will turning,
they will always return to being bees,
ducking in, and out of flowers,
dusting the earth with pollen.

The form of what catches sight,
and the peppered taste,
this body like all bodies, entering the air
alive with sunsets, and perpetual sunrises,
will always return to being a body among bodies.
But what I am
will not return to the sea as seasonal rain.

My cumulative selves

acquired after eating an orange
or the second time at sex, will not return
to its origins to be triangulated,
and sent out again
among the woods, and cities of the world.
I will not find my shadow again
on the ground trailing after me like a dog,
a wounded shadow, a blue star,
a tail wagging in the wind.
But who I am
will blossom
in the New
like a thimble
full of light
or a clear acorn
resting
in the palm of his hand.

# **Our Bluebird Song**

I wish I were a tree
to tie a string around your finger
to remember to wear a ring like water
Halo of evenings we carry through our lives
past the eyes of children in the garden playing
on the harps of clouds they dream
On our backs we dreamt that childhood passing
in the park with swings and slide
and the green leaves burned so brightly
as if to sing praise
For it all was praise and prayer
we just didn't hear it

To set the canoe adrift
on the rippled mirror of a lake in summer
and glide under the lavender glow
as stars began to poke the sky
and to think in this moment
I want to live and never die

As autumn leaves gather at our feet
while a squirrel scampers up the tower of a tree
with the one window facing towards the sea

We have climbed all these years to touch the bell
in the moment that disappears
from the upper sway of branches
like the wind that was the will of our life
now retired to a garden planting bulbs for spring
as we listen to the song in birds sing
our bluebird song.

# Owls in the Canyon

There are deer in the night.

I cannot see them
but hear the cracking of twigs,
the snap of a branch
the scruff across unseen leaves,
as they move up the ridge
through pools of moonlight,
and the thin shadows of branches
that swim across their backs
as they duck nimbly
and pass underneath the foliage.

Owls in the canyon chant their monastery
in clefts of darkness locked away in secret.
Their voices remind us
of the hollowness in our throats
after the burial of a loved one
or downy light softer than water
that we seldom touch in the eyes of the dead.

I reach down to where the small
engines of insects whine in the dark place
under the duff of the forest floor
and touch the stars in the singing, touch
the clear stream in the throat of the moon.

Who believes me in all of this?
At the top of the ridge

in a clearing of trees,
one of the deer has stopped to look back.
Its large ears are translucent receptors
to any hint of fear.
Satisfied,
it disappears from sight.

# Photo Diary

In memory of Theresa Kramer


And what will I bring to death on that day?
Will my pocket be full of coins?
Will I be humming an Edith Piaf song?
Will the headstones
in the cemetery lay down
and become a flat path going into the woods?
All the field mice will dress up in little tuxedos
and attend the funeral under the wood pile
of stacked oak I used for the wood stove.
The old house will be dark at night.
Will they have the sense to turn off the water
up at the well in the apple orchard
or will there be a constant drip in the sink?
How I loved to save old jars
or anything that could contain anything.
There will be
those late October blackberries to be canned.
Will I bring a bowl of fresh berries
and offer them to death on that day?

Will someone offer Cleo, my cat, a warm lap

while they read a book from my bookshelf?
Who will take Cleo in once death
has accepted my bowl of blackberries
and I have stopped humming old tunes in my head?
Some relative, no doubt,
but maybe Cleo will just run off into the woods
to hunt for me
or curl up in a nest of pine nettles.
It has been years since Walter left me,
but then, it was just yesterday
that he first ventured a kiss.
I can still feel the warmth
of his hand in mine as we walked together.
Where will all the photographs of our life together
slip off to when death
comes asking for the change in my pocket?
Will they simply fade in an old shoebox?
My sisters will frame some of them for keeps sake,
but soon their photographs
will also litter the emptiness
inside some box or remain quiet
inside the covers of a photo diary.

# Play This Quiet Place In Me

Play this quiet place in me.
I am sleeping inside a leaf.
Sunlight, play this quite place in me.
October is about to arrive
and the palace of leaves grow gold
in the temple of the orchard.
Play this quiet place in me
with your dark cello.
The crows are on the wind
and gather in the trees.
Please, play this quiet place in me.
Clouds pass by in the sky
and I sail inside.
Oh, play this quiet in me.
Find my lips in the dark
and sing our love
and play this quiet in me.
I want to touch the quiet October in you
as you play the quiet in us.
Your skin is so soft, I barely want to touch
the breath you are.
So sing the quiet in me

and I will play you like a cello in the dark,
sing all praise as to the quiet that you are in me.

# **Praise**

Cormorants bob on the great vast,
unconcerned that a storm rages.
Thrown up on the water worn cliff,
one cormorant snagged by death—the stiff black
wing covering the eyes that saw you God,
sings your praises in life and in death.

# **Prehistoric Windows**

For Jill

An owl out there
near the horse standing
still as night
falls on the meadow.
Steam at the nostrils –
Large brown eyes –
Even before Christ
or the huts of Rome,
the stammering horse.
Out near the pond
in the meadow
those large eyes:

prehistoric windows on the world

# Quiet Within

for Robinson Jeffers


The years I spent
escaping from under your shadow, Jeffers,
that glided over me
like the great wing of the hawk.
In my youth, I was caught by your vision,
but my pride fought off the claws of your words
that snagged my soul. Now I return,
somewhat glad for the traces of prophecy
that gild your thought like the set sun on the Pacific
that gilds the cypress and the pines of Carmel.
That high flicker of youth
has burned the candle down
into a quiet reflection in myself.
I argued Christ with you,
and my verse fought back
at your vision of God.
Now, a deeper surrender, as my wry grin
fades in the mirror like the last light at sunset
fades from the stone house
you built so many years ago.

I now wander into the hills

and lie down to sleep with the shadows,
and the moon over my body, glowing clean.
I walk at dusk with those slender trees,
never to be captured by man or his dream,
and let the roots of my feet
slip into an icy stream.
I lived long, down in the city,
and gagged on chemicals, and a synthetic vision,
a digital empire empty from within; a Wasteland
of lights awash in a spiritual death.

Yet Jeffers,
I come back to you, and smile
at the windfall of apples in the orchard,
and I surrender to all that returns to mother,
and all that is quiet within us.

# <u>Reconciling Copper Pennies</u>
# <u>In The Golden Well</u>

I am surprised by the simplest of things,
a hummingbird dipping its long bill
into the throat of a flower,
sucking on the nectar of heaven.

I wait in anticipation like an expectant mother,
I wait for the storm over the ocean
to break loose
and for waves to thunder into the cliffs.

I am not afraid to receive
the beauty of sorrow and lost suffering
binds my heart to the treasures found in hope
and hope glows like early morning sunlight
on a stream meandering through the woods
in spring.

Joy and sorrow are an open meadow
where deer cross over into the deep woods
and therein the mystery of love
glows in the dark pain we all endure but not alone,

we endure pain and loss
at the communion table of the heart
we break bread and together sing
soft like the birds
and blue bells do ring our common humanity.

# Relative

Albert Einstein yawned and stretched
at his desk cluttered with papers. He decided
a late night walk in the nearby woods
would be refreshing. He crossed a field
to the edge of the woods. It was early Spring.
The grass in the field was tall and glowed silver.

Albert was thinking about the silver light
as he entered the woods by way of a familiar path.
Little did he know, a tick had clambered aboard
his pant leg as he strolled along.

Albert stood in a clearing in the woods
and lit his pipe. There was a brief meteor shower.
The tick, the size of the head of a pin, was slowly
climbing the backstairs of Einstein's leg.
What was relative in all this was the size of the stars
that pricked the night sky and the size of the tick.

Soon, Albert was back at his desk
to finish the last of a calculation

about the nature of light.
He turned off the desk lamp
and slipped under the sheets.
In the dark of the room,
his favorite violin glowed softly
from the moonlight
filtering in through the window.

Einstein's dreams were slightly odd.
Tonight, he dreamed
about gravity bending light
and bicycling down a hill
in his childhood town.
He also dreamed, he was again
with his first wife,
who kept biting him along the soft side
of his groin. In the dream, she had enormous teeth
and was boring a hole into his most private place
like some black hole in space.

In the morning, when he awoke,
he discovered the bloated tick
and realized the nature of his
nightmarish dream.

# <u>Relics</u>

I found a city entirely fashioned
from relics of Rome,
and rooms awash with sea water,
the frescos of childhood
fading into a finite phantom
where rollercoaster thrills had peaked then vanished
into a pharmaceutical underworld of dank sewers
flowing thinly just beneath the eyelids.

# Respite

In the far night a deer, quick as shadow
stops at a brook to drink a gift:
moonlight thins in the silence.
I am adrift with dreams.
I live in these woods
seeking quiet for my soul,
respite from the festival
of my kind clamoring for position
in a machine made more visible
as the sun climbs the hills.
The machine munches on golf balls at lunch,
and deals are made
in which the children are depleted balloons
of helium let loose.
See them sagging with school books
as they enter the machine with a flag
attached to the top, dangling limply
like a dead tiger's tail. Pull on it
with all the dignity you can muster,
but the dead caucus won't budge
unless you wave some money
under its nose to revive
a politician, maybe two

whims that whimper loud,
bang then war.

I listen as the deer slips the stream.
The cleft feet trail up past wide ferns.
I am awake now.
The moon like a large coin
hangs above the hills.
In the morning when the sun
rises in the east
everything here will be alive
in this place of gift.

I will splash my face with water.
Jays will wait on the tree outside
for my stale bread.

The lights of the machine
will have been turned off.
Rows of cubicles lining the asphalt
on both sides will begin
to ring with alarms, bells, and phones.

Here, the tall trees will catch bright wind
in the upper branches. Who understands light?
What can I tell you?

I do not live in the machine.

Early evening, the doe
with her fawn will strip the blackberry vines
of tomorrow's jam.
How can I stop them,
and what do these creatures
give in return?
The machine does not exist in them.
This is their freedom inexplicable, but true,
and yet not a hint of this knowledge lives in them.
Sin is outside their Eden but for us.
We carry the virus into these creature's habitants.
The native tribes moved with the herds,
flow of streams, seasons of light.
The moon for them was not a bright coin.
Their eyes had never witnessed the machine.
Yes, the mountain tribes had the secret of the bow,
and knew of war, but the lower villages
slipped across streams like these deer.

Barely a trace of these people.
Their villages
under the water of Pine Flat Dam.
Sycamore Creek but a dream in minds lost forever.

# **Ritual**

A scrub jay dropped in
on my winter garden, the earth bare
and ready for seed.
The jay found a weathered board
it needed for the hardness of the surface.
I watched as the bird
balanced an acorn between its claw-like feet
and began to peck, peck at the source of things.
Occasionally the acorn would slip from the clutch
and tumble to earth like a coin filled with rain,
but the jay was swift
to snatch back nature's meat.

The pecking beak continued
the ritual of trying to break the shining shell.
Suddenly a Stellar's jay
with its black clairvoyant hood
dropped onto this patch of earth.
The scrub jay abandoned the rapping
and let the acorn fall;
an intruder
had entered the court!

The acorn laid on the open earth.
So this is how oak trees are spread across the hills.

Suddenly I saw the ritual in all things:
the rings at the core of the redwood trees
married to the slow silence of the years,
last year's rain locked in dark
behind the shell of the acorn: something
rapping, rapping at the door,
hungry for the meat of God.

# <u>Roaming the Hills</u>

The road capers slowly with curves

towards the top of the hills.

It is easy to drift off

into an emptiness,

a ravine.

At the bottom

a creek rasps with light

across boulders.

The sun blush

slides off

the Pacific

beyond the range in the west.

Under the canopy of the branches,
                          the leaves are
cool shadows
                for cows.

        My eyes gathered in the surrounding
landscape.

            I was hungry for peace.

        Bird chit, a whir, clouds drifting,
shadows,

                grazing deer in the open,

            a small calf using its mother

            as a shield of flesh against

        a bobcat blending with the
auburn hills,

a wild domain leaning into the
domesticated,

both disappearing and
reappearing

in the untamed

calm

of the bobcat's eyes.

# __Rummaging__

If I cease to exist

and the light in my skull

blinks off like a firefly

will the earth continue

to roam across the seven continents

in search of green orchards and waterfalls?

If I cease to exist

and the heat of my sex

is extinguished in the dark pools of dreams

will Autumn still catch on fire with auburn leaves?

If I cease to exist

and my bones become signatures of dust

will the silkworm become the spider of a storm?

If I cease to exist

and my blood dries at the root of an ocean

will waves cease to lap the shores?

If I cease to exist

will others continue to shower and shave,

prune roses

and will wars disappear and rare perfume

will linger on the air?

If I cease to exist

will you ever read this poem again

or will this become the duff of a forest floor?

# Scarecrow

Eyes follow me through the dark
out into this opening:
a field under the sky.
I am splayed out as if dead,
a scarecrow in autumn fire.
The words in my mouth numb my lips with cold.
Old scarecrow with eyes for buttons,
a straight line for lips,
your heart stuffed into a plaid shirt,
a crow on your shoulders,
cawing in the light.
My heart has been stuffed into dry straw
and set fire by divorce.

# Shadow Tail

(Oklahoma, late October)

Squirrels balanced
on a thin branch.
sunlight, wind and leaves.
Autumn glow in the woods.
A scamper, a leap,
alert black eyes
in the world of the woods.
adrift in a sea of leaves.

The little thieves
give a vertical chase and then leap into open space,
catching the handle of a branch with ease.
She has draped the woods with her scent
and the boys are in a frenzy
for her flower.
They loop the trees and then up and down the trunks
they go in pursuit.
This nonsense is camouflaged by moss
and somber tones.

The shadow dance flits from branch to branch
until she slows in her choice

that
slips in
to her quiet quiver
and leaves her later to her leaf nest
shining in the woods.

# She Is Most Beautiful

Stars above disappear
as storm clouds arrive.
I step out
into the summer night
waiting for her to arrive. She is
most beautiful and shines
when her hair and face
are wet with rain.

# <u>Signs and Wonders</u>

Along the country road
miles and miles of fence crows
perched in their crackle gossip
and some prophetic message
comes in the wind
from off the dry hills of summer
and they all rise up into the sky
like an ominous cloud.
Their shining caws
are a dark symphony
for they perceive the Second Coming
of a storm far off in the distance
that will bring rain to the thirsty hills.

Yet, many prophetic messengers,
Christians with a revelation,
who tend to perceive the unknown hour
as they look for a sign,
not knowing what they see in the ominous cloud
is just a gathering of crows in flight
and the hour in passing just brings the rain
of renewal, so the wildflowers can rejoice
in the bloom of colors.

# Silent Night

Dedicated to 26 children and adults
at Sandy Hook Elementary


Weep hard. Weep long.
Weep out the storm in you.
Pound the walls with your grief.
Throw yourself
over the cliff into sleep.
Become a tide pool of dreams,
dream of your children, dream of her,
and when you wake in a sweat, grip the pillow,
twist it with your anger,
tear at the long sheets of despair.
God doesn't mind. No guilt. No shame.
And when you have wept yourself dry
as the air you breathe,
hold your ache open like a door,
and walk into it. Write the pain of it
with the ink of your soul. In the time to come,
you will have written many letters to her,
and you will read them aloud to her,
on the park playground bench.
You waited for her to come,
holding your swollen belly,

listening for her, feeling the kicks of joy,
laughing with the gals over coffee,
and then came the gift.
Now torn from you
in seconds the world went red
and whimpered as she hid
from the seething one,
detached glow in the eyes,
seeking out a bridge
back to something tangible,
the touch of the mother, all lost now, gone,
what the hell!
Chase down your fear in each hallway
and each room of your remote soul.
Taking their small lives was not enough,
You took your own as well...
The Book of Tragedy opens in hearts of millions
and the pages are barren
like the winter trees.

Weep hard America,
weep for your lost innocence,
weep for your detached sensations
because the apple does not fall
far from the tree.

# Slow Thoughts

The slow thoughts of the earth
begin time, and end time
as thunder erupts in the hills.
Lightning is in the belly of low flying clouds.
A crackling, a bolt of light lashing upward
from that positive patch of earth
or striking the tops of trees with flame,
a shudder into the very thoughts of earth.
Here the earth twists through strata
as sea shelves pushed inland,
rippling the plains into lush green hills,
leaving shell debris,
the skeletal remains of a thriving oceanic life.
No one remembers the time.
No Yokut or Pomo villages on knolls
overlooking geological events;
yet a glimmer of the divine permeated
every rapture of the earth with intense thought
entering even the solid core
past the fires of stone, and lakes of liquid earth.
There was no fear on the earth.
No city.

The earth was a loom, He was weaving
like a passerine bird's woven nest.
The fibers of the earth, the warp,
and the weft of solid sea stone, all earth tones,
and shades of light touched by wildflowers,
and cut by the tumble of clear streams,
and river torrents cutting channels to the sea,
sky touched slate.
No clocks, nothing late. All serene joy,
the slow thoughts of the earth.
Know Him, see Him
as you place a cheek to the sheer rock
faced serpentine cool flame frozen in time.
Hear His thought as you touch
the star glazed granite.
I sit here, a thought crouched on a slit of sheer
wind fall slant of earth.


I had followed a deer trail along the edge
through handsome trunks of madrones,
and bearberry.
First there was the climb up
through the Bad Land's heat of the March sky
ironed blue, and scorching.
Each foot was placed carefully

in the crumble of crushed earth.
I was grateful for the easy switchback trail
of the graceful creature.
I'd found hoof prints marking the earth.
No doubt this one was on the scent of water
that rustled in the creek below.
A little cascade of stone,
then a silence within a silence,
for I was calm in my being,
and content when I found a perch
high as the hawk's shadow
that touched this sheer hike.
It was here that I took breath,
and found my life for a moment
folding itself into the hills
formed before humankind knew the creation.
I'd climbed up here away from my kind:
those who fashioned stones into tools,
and from pueblo to suburban sprawl,
they became the conquistadors out of Spain,
out of Silicon Valley with manicured lawns.

A gentle touch fills

this hallowed niche in a cleft of rock.
I am glad to look down through the valley,
and let my eyes feast on the vista,
simply grateful at full sight,
and the modest bit of this life lingering.

# South County

for Ed Callons


A warm night…
I think on the old oak off in the dark
twisting up into the stars,
clear air,
insects in all their sounds
talking, a small breeze,
my longing to be one with all this,
enter the silence,
and journey inward into that place
of listening to God
here in the hills of South County.
They say ancient sea shelves pushed inland,
and rippled the flat
into the roll of dells catching water.
But here, under the great oak alongside the road,
on the other side of Ed's barbed fence,
the oak looms up into a black
that catches the glint of stars.

"What do you like best, Ed,
living out here on six thousand acres?"

That slow reply: "Well, I like the stars.
You can see the stars."
His body is taut. The eyes a soft blue,
but you know his eyes are on you,
wise, and subtle as a wind in the trees.
His eyes are taking me in.
They say the Greeks
did not count books for much worth,
but rather thought the better of oral tradition.
Too much value placed on the book
rather than its content,
Better to talk than to read.
It was good talking to Ed about the land,
and how on a clear night
the stars were alive in his mind.
He read cowboy books
by an author who wrote in the 20's.
I did not catch the author's name.
I did manage to write Ed's name down
on a scrap of paper
when I climbed back into my truck.
I'm almost certain
the old oak will survive our names,
and our brief talk alongside the road.

# <u>Stains</u>

Some of us

Are between two or three worlds

There is so much weeping here

I cannot find one leaf

That is not stained

By tears

# **Stare Out**

A body is

in an old hotel.

There is a cricket under the bed

blessing the silence

inside a turned over shoe.

The face on the body is like glass.

There is no replica of this face in all the world.

The eyes in the face do not see.

The mind in the head has drifted away,

evaporated like rubbing alcohol.

There was nothing else for the eyes to do,

but to stare out the open window.

# **Storm**

Grove, Oklahoma


The night follows the night like a river
in the dark window, which is passing.
A storm, all lightning, all thunder
has strewn black-boned branches across the road;
a wet ribbon rising and falling
through the roll of fields.
The fields stretch long and wide in the open silence
and drifts off into decay
to where the black fence of trees silhouette the sky.

In the aftermath of the storm, the heavens shine.
A pond mirrors the stars. Fish nip at the surface
thinking the stars are small insects.
Here, the raw furry
had tested the tessellation of nature.
Now the ponds and lakes are a shimmer of calm.
A few fireflies blink in the woods.
The heart gets lost in prayer
as clouds drift past a full moon.
But off in the east the storm still blinks softly
with lightning

and the trees nearby go dark to light, to dark
with each distant flickering...
my life of trials and delights
blinking on and off
in my soul.

# **Streams of Sunlight**

Sunlight touching every lake,

mirror, strand of hair,

window, puddle, river, meadow,

spoon on a morning table,

faces in cars at rush hour, eyes of cows, dogs, cats,
lizards, fish,

insects, human, sort of human, snake eyes, beetle
eyes, hummingbird eyes,

fish scales, leaf, slanting through redwoods,

filling hotel windows,

doorways half in shadow, towers of granite,

empty classroom, empty heart,

jubilance minds,

moments in math,

the equation and equality

of the democratic dream.


America is a European dream.

Walt Whitman was the true face of that dream,

the utopian dream,

and I hear the voice of that dream

as a splinter of sunlight that stretches

across this vast land

from the vertical towers of Manhattan,
across the quiet prairies, slipping
through the snow peaks of the Rockies,
to touch the lip of a wave about to break
on a reef on the horizontal West.

We have a dream, and it is still strong within us
like the icicles of sunlight that cannot be broken.

# Summer Lingers

Summer lingers on in the length of the last wind.

October sun waits in the skirts of leaves.

As the apples in the orchard ripen into golden
delicious.

Storms are far out at sea but soon enough

the ragging of waves will come

and the dry riverbeds will become torrents of water.

But now is the time of flowers and of bees

that move in and out of the Kingdom in bloom,

the way the Lord moves in us

and then out into the world.

As he sails his Light

on candled ships

into the harbors of other hearts.

# The Face Once Green

The face once green leaf fine as pure fire
Now like a crumpled moon
An autumn leaf
Found on a bridge crossing
From dawn to dawn

A tear lost in the mirror of remembrance
Her lover unbuttoning her blouse in spring
Has all but disappeared except
For his tobacco pipe he left behind
And one shirt still hanging in her closet

Every Sunday the daughters bring
The grandchildren
Their laughter is the gift of water
Quenching the thirst of lonely hours
When she stands alone in the kitchen
The only light in the dark is an open refrigerator

She still sleeps on one side of the bed
Half expecting to feel him slip under the covers
Where small bells of her dreams are ringing

On the other side of her soft breathing

Between the soul and the body
There is the mystery
That plays itself out like a silent film
She dreamed herself to be Louise Brooks
Those alluring eyes and flutter of charm
But her name was Susan from Kansas City
Her smile all but faded
A leaf that had fallen
On the bridge between two dawns

# The Moment

I was a strong wind in the bed of my lover
until she closed the curtain
and night fell on our bodies.
Then I discover the secret
of the candle flame
and the wind outside the window.

Men are weak and cannot find their wings
inside her breathing.

Even an apple is stronger than a man
who looks too long into her eyes.

The branch is meant to carry the leaves
out onto the balcony of the sun.

The lake carries the sky around all day like a mirror.

Cloud shadows drift across the hills
like our dreams until the morning.

Kiss her once and you will understand history.

The second kiss will build into a house

and the third will bring the laughter of children.

So if life is an accordion, who is the player?

I cannot count that far.
It is irresistible as water to think I could
count all the stars in the night sky.

A pulsar burst like a belly full of light.
Christ was walking around the towns of Galilee
at the moment it occurred
and that light has just now reached your eyes.

Is this the way love reaches us from the beginning
of the past to the moment the light
first shined in her eyes?

Why play the countess in an evening gown
borrowed from your cousin?
It is better to lose your slippers in the dark
then to be pursued by the betrayal of a lothario.

I touch the hem of water and it is music to the touch.

I touch your cheek in the night
and it is like the warmth of silk
spun from the moonlight.

Children are the puzzle we play
with each kiss of fire…
soon we begin to see the picture forming
and one relative whispers, she has your eyes.

# The poem was waiting for me today

as I drove the back hills
along the narrow curves.
Hollister heat had turned the hills
from green to dry. Cattle found shade
under great oaks,
snakes in the cool hollows between stones,
I had my wide-brimmed hat,
and the window rolled down as I shifted the gears
down into a stretch of fields,
and orchards where the migrant workers bent down
laboring next to the heat.
Stopping at Tres Pinos Creek,
the poem took me in
like the eyes of a woman,
and I followed her warm flow.
Wildflowers, and the wind
crowning
everything with a quiet fire
burning towards the core of beauty.

A silence here
except for the rattle of thistle.

# The Thief and The Poet

for Joseph Stroud

I am the thief that broke into your cabin
along Shay Creek
that was frozen over with black ice.
I had wandered out of the woods,
Hungry for civilization: coffee, cigarettes,
and your corn whiskey.
I had taken the trackless path into Cold Mountain,
and after years of hermitage among the pines,
and cedars,
I longed for a dwelling among men.
When I first caught sight
of the neatly stack firewood on the porch,
I approached your dwelling like a wary bobcat.
The cabin stood there,
a silence within the silence of the white wind.
A flurry began to fall,
and with my face lifted upward,
I could taste heaven melting on my tongue.
How quickly these snowflakes melt on my tongue
like our lives open to the solitude, open to the thief,
and the poet:

the quiet one reading ancient verse,

and the crafty one.
When I entered your dwelling,
I cared little for your poems,
but rather put them to better use by burning them
to set the kindling wood ablaze,
and letting your logs roast
until they became hot embers in the dragon's eyes.
Your whiskey warmed my mind
with a dull sleep. I was old now,
and could not use the stars
to guide my travels through the wilderness
of the Northern Sierra,
and when I found your compass,
I was thankful because I knew I could find my way
back to all that I loved,
and the gold of dusk
embedded in quartz.

# The Wild November Wind

I waited all night at the small window
that opens to the dark. I was listening into myself
the way one listens to the surf inside a conch shell.

No one knows the One who gives life.
The stream out in the woods flows quietly
under the moon.
The One who gives life is life.

Deer slip down a trail into an opening,
seeking the wild November wind.

My father died. No one knows where he went
after he closed his eyes on the soft light of death.

Only the One who gives life and death knows
where he went seeking wild November wind.

Down past the canyons, gorges
and ravines, to where small waves break
in a quiet cove.
He had to go. I know he had to go. For a man,

Eighty-four is considered a long life. But for me,
I would re-wind the reel and start over to what ever
starting over is…
a perennial that finds its colors again?
Is there really a new moon
at the bottom of a rain barrel?

He was so handsome and robust,
but the wild wind sought him out
and took him without notice. I don't want to write
concise words about death or his life.

It is a hard thing to know that we are dust
or like a cloud
with a glint of sun, we move along,
only to disappear.

I cannot believe that this thing death has struck
again.
First my brother, my friend's eldest son,
took the tragic line,
the lure of vodka
and the barbed hook just gutted him.
There was no mercy in the clear vodka
and the celebration of life
stained the lips with the last drink.

They could not bring him back
and the wild wind took him.
The next day,
his wife had me hold her
as she trembled and wept.
Her wet cheek touched mine like an innocent kiss.
She kept repeating over and over
like she was rubbing a rosary,
"Just yesterday we were fighting and I cursed him."
She said this
like I could lower her down into a small boat
and row her across the lake to the day before,
and she could have been kinder,
and untie the harsh words
stitched into the caw of the crow,
but judgment is madness and cannot be unsown
once it is stitched into the wild November wind.

He is gone like our father.
No words can catch up to death.
No way to redo yesterday once it has been rehearsed
in the mirror of memory.
No way to say I am sorry or stroke the thin hair,
hear an old joke, talk about the war years,
laugh over dinner
while passing the potatoes.

The wild wind of November has entered the house.
Waves in the cove break along the shore.

…gently death, gently ease us
down

through our pain…

I asked his wife of 58 years,
how it was with her.
She missed the warmth of him next to her at night,
and she would awake in the dark and weep a little
and hope for sleep…

…gently death, gently, ease us down

through our pain…

# The Winter Wind

The winter wind
is about to arrive
and the nights of winter ocean storms dashing
the cliffs where cormorants perch
in their cubbies undisturbed
at the fury unleashed.

October is still perched
on the golden windowsill
and the blackberries
have ripened with the sun
as do the windfall of apples,
golden as well,
that litter the orchard floor.

All these years
I have watched
as the lessons of the seasons like Braille to my eyes,
open to the quiet
dark of evenings.

No storms here tonight,
Only the perfume of stars
lingering in the garden.

To sit here in this quiet
and look across the centuries...
To know that

the scent of war
has no place here,
only the hummingbird with its music...
A filament the moon uses
as it rises above
the river hills.

## Tonight, I want to sleep close to the earth

where the snail crawls along
the moist latitude of silence

carrying its house around like a lantern of pale light.

I want to be found under the roses in the dark garden

glowing like a patch of moonlight.

Here the cat waits like a coiled spring

ready to surprise anything that moves out there,

and those eyes under the bushes

are two small globes of green fire.

I want the grass so close to my face

that each blade becomes a transparent window

slipping through the pores of my skin.

# **Too Quickly**

Your eyes never again can visit
the countryside of your youth
when the streams ran clean, and your small feet
endured with joy the suck of mud
at the water's edge
where bright things swam quickly
through your sight
in that fast water more translucent than a dream.
Too quickly this passed.
The tree-house swing,
and how she hung onto the two huge ropes,
leaning back as she kicked out over space,
and swung back up into the sky;
the old sycamore branch creaked lightly
with the memory of her weight,
and her squeal of joy quietly
that disappeared on the wind.

# To Tag New Butterflies
# To Help Her Sleep

I was floating down a well full of rainwater.

My body was a compass pointing every direction

like a nova in a drop of ink.

I was nailed inside a leaf falling
towards a familiar dream.

The blood in my veins is a triumph in defeat,
laughter within water,
a siren in the night looking for the heart.

Sea horses pull my carriage
towards the museum of the impossible.

I set sail to find the source of all books,
only to drop anchor
in a cove the size of the Milky Way.

Hip-Hop across the scratch on the mirror
and after a hot day in the fields,

drink long and deep the music of the watermelon.

There are no moments
moving inside of the mountain moist

as a sponge of seaweed cucumber blue.

I do not wish to follow the goldfish up the stairs
to where the stars

begin to bloom into planetary wishes
and voyages and the mind

gone movie and blue ray.

This odd way of writing words to slant sideways
like a beam

of light bouncing off surfaces.

The traffic is a blur of headlights
and streaks of neon cotton candy.

She painted her long nails
with the colors of Las Vegas

and then stretched out like a sand dune under the
desert moon

while pharmaceutical companies
continued to coin gentle

nomenclatures
and tag new butterflies
to help her sleep.

# **Tornado**

What if sunlight were cold as fish scales
and moonlight, the warmth of baked bread?

What if the queens worked for the ants
and landlords could not collect rent?

What if all the bunglers with guns
could not find ammunition,
would the world turn into one colossal mistake
or would whales and songbirds
sing in a language that humans could comprehend?

This will be the day that lions lose their claws
and tornados unwind into a peaceful sleep.

# Totem

In the Book of Grief, I light a candle.
Many of the faces in here
are Stories of Innocence,
but that is another book
in which the ant hill has not been trampled,
and the simple fly is something of beauty.

In the Book of Grief a whole human history is lost
like the red, white, and blue Pepsi label
fading on a piece of aluminum
under a tropical sun. Once
the tribe here
drank cool rainwater
from a catch of large leaves. Now
they are off at the recycling center
trying to cash in on aluminum cans.

And who labors long
reading The Book of Grief?

Here at the heart of the book,
the hind brain stands like a totem
entwined with a quiet storm.

# Tracking the Bear

Black edges of a frozen stream…
drifts of snow…
small tracks skitter white powder,
trail off into blank trees.

To have journeyed through passes,
across plains, picking wild flowers…
to end behind winter Wyoming door
with an enraged husband
is not wisdom
but a fact that endures
in man,
a pain
that turns the woman
against him,
and even the horse resents the spur
as it moves against the high snow drifts,
tracking the bear.

# Translator of the Heart

I wanted to tell someone
about my sins. I even
went so far as to pay,
and put my meager offering
in the basket that was passed
from hand to hand like a bribe.
And just to sit for an hour or so
listening to the pitch of a car salesman
was not enough. I was indeed
the man they had been looking for
throughout the centuries.
Had I not committed every atrocity?
The criminal mind lurked in me.
I had given in on numerous occasions
to all sorts of debauchery,
yet I remained. And
in the moment of confession,
he laughed while shaving in a small mirror
that was a pocket of clear water
at the edge of the cold stream.
The tall alder caught the wind,
and whispered light along the banks.

My face was the face in the mirror.
Again I repeated my guilt, and shame,
even listed my faults alphabetically
thinking an orderly list would get a blessing
or possibly a merit, but that is when she
started to vacuum, and the phone rang,
and the jays screeched at each other
over their own territory of sin.
Then I saw it. Laughing, I saw it,
the terrible reason, and why one child
yanks the toy from the other child
when both have a yard full of toys.
It is splendid that the dentist can't keep up
with decay, and the earth is in constant retrieval
even if the dinosaur is extinct, attempting
to mend the torn fabric so simply intricate
as to take billions of cells to produce
one utterance, one confession, one depiction
in the mind of blemish. Yes, that in, and of itself
is why I laugh through my own abstractions
because this existence is layered with infirmities
edging towards perfection like a priceless book
in mint condition just gathering dust,
never open. If we open a stone
from the clear running stream,
we will see the glitter of stars,

and if we open an old oak, entering
we will know a stillness
that surrounds God's name.

I stopped the car, and turned off the headlights.
Under the roll of hills, the hum of insects.
A meteor streaks the night like a small spark,
and is forever gone.
I touch the rough bark of the old oak,
and I begin to open like a book:
inside are some recognizable codes.
Suddenly the whole landscape enters me,
and I am no longer fearful
for inside the old oak was nailed
a name in blood that translates Father,
Forgiver, and Translator of the Heart.

# Tree Frogs and Joy

The Sierra Tree Frogs mating calls are blocked
by the passing of cars
in the night
as the surf breaks
into the cliffs.

A young couple walking – talking – laughing,
exploring each other in that weave of innocence.

As they walk by, I mentioned the tree frogs
and their mating calls
and they thought
I'd lost my marbles as they used to say.

No, I'm listening to Sierra Tree Frogs
and their symphony in the tall moist grass
singing their mating song...

Like flowers sing with pollen,
and hummingbirds sing with nectar,
and children's laughter, is the seed
of their beginning...

I hear the young couple laughing in the distance
and their laughter fading
as the mist from the ocean closes in
on a deeper dream
and a silence of beauty
there in. . . . Such Joy.

# **<u>Trinity</u>**

Three white egrets
rising and falling,
drifting in perfect grace
above the still lake flying
in a music of their own,
aloof from our kind.
Their shadows touch
the surface of the water,
the three white egrets;
the trinity
of one.

# **Truth**

There are roads in this earth
that follow into night,
and are covered with blood.

Someone grabbed
the end of a tablecloth,
and pulled an entire century into chaos.

Eyes blink on barbed wire.

A white-hot cinder burns
through the child's cheek
all the way into the kingdom come.

Tell me about logic.

The spring iris
glows blue. Is this the flame
that burns in the soul?

We are a cruel species.

Look into the eyes of the child after Napalm.

The straight line is a device
that has held for centuries.

This woman Mary followed Him
to the outskirts of time,
to the edge
of our cruelty that mark us human creatures
that must turn to Him or die.

In Him is Truth, and raison d'être.

*ray-zawn det-tra*  (Fr. : reason for being)

# <u>Two Edges</u>

Near the fence field
mice scramble across the white glare,

headlights sudden as death
hit the dash of wild
across the windshield, and rain.
The warm deer split open
to all that it is:
mist at the nostrils,
the final look,
not helpless,
no goodbye,
but something in it
takes you closer to what we are,
that black stare that arches neurons, and stars,
the final look back at you
beckoning for you to follow forever into serene,
and final peace.

The traffic slows
passing the scene in the night
near the woods, near the city,
the two edges of winter beauty.

# Under The Light Of Stars

A highway somewhere in America
slips off into the quiet wildflowers.
Fireflies drift above the black asphalt
near the fields where William Blake
is pulling the night down around us,
speaking into our dreams
of how giant stars go whistling
through the tall, solid earth with its roll of hills
catching on fire with the light of the moon,
and white deer glide off
under the light of stars.

# Understand

The blue iris ambles up its stem
to where the rain shines on the lips of February.

She is out on the deck
that overlooks the San Lorenzo River,
flowing brown in a race to the sea.

It rained all night.
We awoke in our small cabin to the sound of it all.
She was restless. Something
in her was racing towards the future.
I heard her slip out onto the deck
and into the night to have a pensive cigarette.

Her mother had called that evening
to stir the kettle of anguish once again.
She was the commander and chief
and she had a strategy. I knew
she had no power. The rain
would keep falling and the muddied water
of the river would continue to flow
towards the openness of the sea.
She had no power to rescue her daughter's

two children adrift in the events of life.

The fostering of the children
leaned towards adoption.
The short term was flowing into the long term.
There seemed no way to stop the flow of water.
The mother offered no words of comfort,
only an empty plan. No long and deep hug
that would reach down into her daughter's pain.

I can only pray that the lips of February
kiss her gently and the blue iris shining with rain
gives her hope in this drift of events
towards winter's end.

# Unspeakable Joy

The moon in the woods.
A quiet that goes all the way
into the light...a lingering.
Listening into this without a thought. Clear tonight
all the way down to the sea. The water
glows. It is
so still I can hear
the bark of sea lions on black rocks.
I cannot see them huddled together.
I know they are there.
They do not know that on a distant ridge
I hear the language of dark kelp in their bark.
They are not concerned about me.
A meteor strikes a match on the deep above.
I glance up and see the hem of the vast Milky Way,
a glaze of light.
There is a joy in me
so deep
that the root of it
touches the garment of Christ,
and the eternal realm
forever.
I have watched as storms from off the Pacific

ripped old oaks from the earth by the roots
and scatter trees, in one night,
that have stood for a hundred years.
Nothing can uproot this joy
I have in Him.
The fury of the wild is calmed with two words,
"Be still."
Tonight
I walk in this stillness, in this unspeakable joy.

# Visit to the Dentist

I look up past the handheld light,
the whir of a small drill inside my mouth,
and study a Van Gogh print tacked to the ceiling.
Gold cypresses like flames lick a blue sky.
There is a vineyard in the distance,
a shaft of light out of the blue
and white smudge of oils.
The light is divine, out of place
from the other knife strokes,
and falls on one lone cypress. I think of him,
alone in himself thinking he is going mad. Trying
to find a language
that would take him into the world
where he could listen to things.

A dry glare is in the small town.
St-Rémy in early autumn.
There is hospital cots, and a wood burning stove.
His brother Theo, buying every canvas
and cluttering his house.

Traps hanging in the air
as he stepped out into the light.

Van Gogh, snagged on despair burned for life.

I listen to the drill and smell burnt bone.
Leaning back in the chair looking up into his world
I discover my own world:
trees outside the window shine,
the tooth sailing in my mouth touches a nerve,
the walls are like new rain. Suddenly
I hear a voice above my head saying,
"You are all done."
Oddly, I thank the dentist
for the pain that translated the air
into a canvas of light.

# Voting

The dark trunks of redwoods
Grow upward singing in their own water.
Everything here in the woods
Is in silence. The wind sifts through the garments
Of the trees. And bees are lost
In the invisible strictures of nature.
We are  but the witness of that which is
Beyond our scope. In the creek bed, dark pools
Of water in a deep linguistics dream, a permeation
Of what is real and what is not.
We are the temporal visitors.
The redwoods are not and will be
Standing long after our house becomes dust.
They are vying for a president of this land.
I am not. I vote for pollen and the unseen mystery.
I vote for the ferns with their green fans.
I vote for that which will remain
And not for the Republic that will not stand.

# Warding Off the Crow

There is stillness here.
I stand
listening
into everything that is alive.
A red-wing blackbird darts upward
from the rush that conceals a nest,
pushing back the crow that is like a glider
drifting backwards with full extended wings.
At first I thought the smaller bird to be
the infant of the larger
but the gist was a simple warding off,
protection hardwired into the
small bird with red medals pinned at the shoulders.
The crow gave off its dark syllabic caw,
and flew off. The blackbird came back
perching on a wavering reed of rush.
Off in the distance
the heat wavering above the fields,
a low murmur of migrant workers
hoeing between the rows of green sprouts of garlic:
the faint laughter mingled with Spanish,
and the blackbird blowing on his small trumpet,

a deep throated whistle known only to its kind.

I climb back into my pickup kicking up a little dust.
In front of me on the road,
a squirrel darts out of nowhere in existence.
My rearview mirror
tells me nature has its timing.
I want to listen into this
but the small pain in my chest
tells me my time will come to pass soon enough.
I wanted to turn around, and undo this thing,
but I missed my chance at integrity
unlike the blackbird warding off the crow.

# <u>Water</u>

As the day grew long with light,
I hiked back into the other life
of wilderness shining with leaves,
alive with oaks,
squirrels that hoard
the hard stuff of nature in round cheeks,
and the red signature of madrone.

The hot spring along the Big Sur River
is what drew me from my city dwelling,
and the desire to be free from constraint.
But as the trail dove long into wilderness
my throat longed for water.
Each leaf of bay and oak
burned like fire on my eyes.
At that moment
my empty plastic water bottle
was as useless as the industry that produced it.

Down below at the bottom of the ravine,
the Big Sur River bulged with rainwater.

My throat crawled with the rasp of dry leaves.
Water flavored my dream like tea.
Everything around me glistened
not with water but with afternoon heat.
Around each bend in the trail
I thought to find a small spring
nestled into a spot of hillside green,
but only large boulders,
broke in on silence
cut by the river below,
and the menace of jays
hoping from one dry stone to another
as if to mock my thirst.

When I did find water
the taste of it was more than joy.
I pressed my face into the icy cold of it
and drank deep the gift
that stills minds.
This gift, this slide of clear water
over stones,
through the flags of green
met my mind and won.
Water taught me
how closely it held my life.

I filled my plastic bottle to the brim,
knowing that without water
the city would hike back up into wilderness
to taste the life it gives.

# When the State Rules

for Kimberly, a wonderful mother
to her children


I took the coast road. There was a break in the storm
and in between it all, I took leave of the town.

I crossed over into an unhurried silence.
The roll of hills on one side
and on the other side, the cliffs
that dropped down into the surge of the Pacific.

I sought the wild impenetrable solace of water.
Huge waves razed the shoreline. Creeks
were swollen with five days of down pour
and cut channels to the open sea. I also
wanted to cut my way out into the open world.

The bureaucrats had taken her children. The State
took her two small flowers. No longer
can she tuck them into bed with a kiss and prayer.
The State took her two small flowers.

She is asleep and dreams in the slowed realm of
Seroquel.

She sleeps past the morning into the afternoon.
I let her sleep in the cabin by the river.
I know she also wants to cut her way out
into that open place
of dreams beyond the reach of pain.

The State had taken her two small flowers.

I stand on the beach. The high tide brings
a slip of white surf up to my feet.
It is beginning to rain. I look up.
My eyes shine with the wet.
I ask God the questions, we all ask God
when deceit and cunning thrive

and the State rules against the mother
and takes her two small flowers.

# Where Light Begins The Tree

for Steve McVey

There is the grackle of blackbirds.
Shadows in the orchard shine.

Do the birds think of us,
as we ponder the birds?

Does the light begin out there?
Does the grackle of blackbirds begin out there?
And if the birds, and the light begin out there
why come indoors at all? But you see
it takes a walk out past the noise of the town,
it calls for getting out of the car,
and strolling without a motive or a destiny.
You just stop, stand and listen.
That's when you hear
what you've been waiting to hear
all your life.

Dad took us kids
to the ocean for the first time.
We tripped over ourselves getting out of the car,
and just stood there listening, and watching

like Mary, mother of Jesus
was walking on the water.
It was as if we realized for the very first time
we were alive in a vast place that our small minds
could not put a name on or speak. I think
that is where the light begins the trees.
As for the grackle, dad said, it was God
speaking through the birds,
and sort of laughing at us,                    ·
not mockingly, but gently,
because we knew so little, and didn't stop to listen,
and catch the glint of light in the blackbird's eye.

# Where The Dark Eddies In The Rush

Stillness mirrors the stars.
Black birds snap clean,
and dart in swarms above the fields.
Some birds carry red jewels on their shoulders
unlike the hawk who blends with the tone of earth.
Other small birds have breast of yellow fire.
The river hills and dells go green with rain.
Night slips in with the surge of surf.
Creeks and streams go down into the quiet of ocean,
and shoreline tide-pools catch stars with clear nets.
Out on the dark kelp forest, petrels
let loose their speech,
and chatter on the roll of swells.
It is the ocean canyon miles deep
that brings sea creature closer in
to where the dwellings of men
dot the night with their window light,
farm house, and fields along the coast highway.
The beams of a car round a curve far off
in the dark where the sea walls rise to meet the trees:
the bark of seals, hiss in the gleam of sea boulders,
moonlight on the stream in the deep of night.
A fingerprint here

no one can decipher like bark peeled
from the trunk of a fallen Douglas Fir,
and along the inside of the bark insects
have carved their cuneiform trail in silence.

# Who's The Faithful One

Did I create the tides that are faithful to the moon
or the roll of waves at night that touch the shores?
Did I establish the sun?
With one hand, do I raise the winds
and cause the storms?
Who is the faithful One
who walks the waters at night,
and are not His words a fire that burns in our hearts
as His faith and love is revealed.

Faith is like lifting stones in the woods
and underneath, you discover yourself
in the mystery being explored,
which is unfathomable.

Did I create the unfathomable?
Did I create the stone with stars shining
in that inner dark?
The woods with the stream aglow with the wind
from off the hills
is the hills with the wind flowing
down into the woods
where we dream the woods. Did I create the dream?

To be the dream of God expressed.
To be the poem of His divine love.
Inescapable…faith
in the One who loved us before we were.

# **Wife**

A fox sniffs the edges of the woodlands.
Crickets are chirping in the tall grass.
Moons eye the ground,
casting clear light through the owl's eye
and branches of white oak.

A canopy of leaves
throws shadows across your body
engraving your moist skin with an ancient design.

I pull your thighs across the slippery moss
into a cold, clear stream.
Our breathing becomes one;
a secret language of water
moving between stones.

The map of our hands;
a journey of transparent veins
drifting to the heart of a pond.

And I, the hunter, have found my own body,
as I tremble over your lips.

The crickets listen in the tall grass
to a horse that neighs in a distant field.

# Wildfires Are Burning In California

Here, the full moon burns softly,
gilding the leaves of black oak with white light.

Thousands flee their homes.

I hear wild geese over the dark lake.
Their cry on the cold air migrates towards
some invisible call.

If we all could flee our burning bodies
and fly home.

# William Blake

A highway somewhere in America
slips off into quiet weeds.
Fireflies drift above the black asphalt
near the fields
where William Blake is pulling the night
down around us, speaking into our dreams
of how giant stars go whistling above
the tall, solid earth
with its roll of hills on fire
with the light of the moon,
and white deer glide off under the stars;
clearness is everywhere at once.

Trees, streams, and little animals
are cut out of cardboard,
and painted by children,
who lay in the grass.

This is too much for the adults,
who march out into the field,
and shake the children
from their dreams:

Time for math, the ideal, and the machine.

# **Willow Creek**

is a rustle of light that flows clean.

On the green knoll above the creek are several oaks:
one great oak. It is late November. A chill has set in.

The grass on the knoll is like green rain,
slender as the fingers of children.

Large flat rocks litter the earth beneath the great oak.
Acorns are everywhere.
This was the place where natives with pestles
pounded the round holes in the flat rocks.

I let my fingers reach down
into the smooth round holes touched with lichen.
I was searching for the nobility of a lost people.
I was searching for myself redefined
by the inscrutable message laid on this place:
a small valley between ridges.

When was it that they lit fires
by the creek at evening?
Even then the young oak's canopy of thick branches
would seem to hold up

the night sky pricked with stars.
Who were the women that found
the rhythm of stone,
and ground the acorns to powder?
What was their will, and their song?

The grass on the knoll
would not give up their names.
The creek below flashed with light,
and the shadows in the hills deepened with dusk.
A heron still as scripture stood in the shallows.
I too was listening under the great oak
for the slightest clue of their presence,
the simplicity they brought
to this grassy knoll by Willow Creek.

# **Wind and Ice**

They were frozen shadows
trying to walk out of time
but ice burned the lips black
and there was no escape,
no huge summer in which to hide
as their squinting faces faded in old photographs.

Their youth was a zither lost in the dead weeds,
tall as a winter wind
and the green lake was frozen over like clear steel.
Off in the distance black trees raised their branches
to the sky
like mourners at a funeral,
chanting, "Their day has passed."

That was in 1911 in a small village. Only yesterday
it seems like but the sensation of it all is gone
and the eyes that saw light are gone
and the village and the main road are gone.

Only a few of the trees remain
and in the spring the leaves return

and in summer there is a green glory in the branches
swaying
gently over the unseen and unmarked graves
of those who once danced in a circle
marking time with each sprint
of their merry-making,
ironic in its liquid and as suddenly gone
to wind and ice and weather not so nice or neat
like that evening they spent up in the orchard
on fire with moonlight
and her eyes were bright
with a dark light that glowed;
gone now her touch
and ache of love.

# Winter Thought

December in Oklahoma


Moonlight ripples at the edge of the lake
like my life rippling at the edge of this existence.
The black oaks will still be standing
when I am gone. I wish them luck.
All my petty thoughts and debts
will vanish like the chatter of ducks
out on the dark lake.
The winter cold touches my face.
I smile. I am alive to this place
and grateful for the brevity
of the one pained thought
that teaches that kindness
is noble and is the crown of consciousness
as the wind takes the flowering stars
and folds them into dust.

# Your Face

Your face invisibly written,
forms a flower's scent
blown from the palm of my hand,
nectar in the wilderness
where I wander past puddles left by a spring shower,
along a cobbled street that shines wet.

There in the puddle
I see your eyes
and I gaze long into your love
mirrored in the image
that shimmers on the surface of water.